THE BEGINNER'S GUIDE TO CHICKEN BREEDS

The BEGINNER'S GUIDE TO CHICKEN BREEDS

AN INTRODUCTORY GUIDE TO CHOOSING THE RIGHT FLOCK

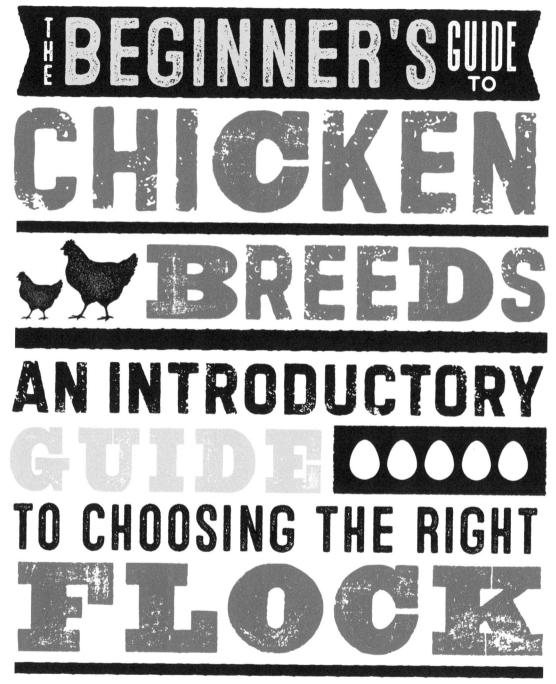

AMBER BRADSHAW

ROCKRIDGE
PRESS

Interior and Cover Designer: Erik Jacobsen
Art Producer: Sara Feinstein
Editor: Brian Sweeting
Production Editor: Matthew Burnett
Production Manager: Martin Worthington

Illustrations © 2020 Annalisa Durante and Marina Durante, cover, p. ii, vi-vii, 1, 3, 4, 31, 42-43, 51, 53, 69, 73, 81, 83, 93, 102, 111, 116, 134; © 2019 Benlin Alexander, p. 7, 11, 22, 39, 50, 61, 134; iStock p. i, iii, 2, 8, 20, 29, 48, 58, 70, 78, 86, 96, 108, 121.

ISBN: Print 978-1-64876-675-6 | eBook 978-1-64876-172-0
R0

TO MY HUSBAND, TIMMY, AND OUR THREE
CHILDREN, GAVIN, MORGAN, AND LINDEN.

CONTENTS

INTRODUCTION: PICKING THE PERFECT BREED

**M**any people are flocking to stores and shopping online to become first-time chicken owners. People who never thought about raising chickens increasingly want to get connected to their food source and raise backyard chickens for a more sustainable lifestyle. Others have been raising their own flock for years but are now interested in owning different breeds.

Deciding to raise chickens is one thing, but figuring out what breed or breeds will best suit your needs is another—and is perhaps not so straightforward as one might think.

Don't know what I mean? No one knows exactly how many chicken breeds there are, but estimates suggest there may be more than 500 different breeds of chickens. Some of these breeds are meant for colder climates, while others thrive in the heat. Some will fill your baskets with eggs, while others are fast growers for meat production. Some are suited for showing at the local fair, and others aren't. Some have a docile temperament, while others are flightier or more aggressive. Picking the right breed can make or break a flock.

Finding the perfect breed for your homestead will be much easier with the proper research and resources. This book, written for both aspiring chicken owners and those who have been raising them for years, will help you assess your needs and guide you in making the best decisions possible about your flock.

We'll cover the best purebreds and hybrids, the best layers and broilers (and the breeds that can do both), the best chickens for beginners, brooding, and much more. For each category of chicken, the book provides an ultimate breed list, highlighting top breeds and breaking down their unique qualities and strengths and the key considerations of owning them. This book also offers cost examples of raising your own flock.

When I first embarked on my chicken journey as an adult, I knew I needed a breed that would thrive in the heat and wouldn't fly the coop on our tiny coastal homestead. I also knew I wanted chickens that were good egg-layers, but at the time, I didn't fully realize all the additional considerations that come with raising chickens. I had to use multiple resources to find the information I needed, and there were still a few things—like breed specifics, climate, and personality traits—that I didn't find in my extensive research that I wish I would have known before I started. I wanted to write a book that provides, in one place, all the information you need to make the best choices for your homestead.

By the time you've finished reading this book, you'll know which breeds possess the traits you're looking for. You will find the best breeds that suit your needs and homestead so you can begin raising your flock or add to an existing one.

CHAPTER 1
WHICH BREED IS RIGHT FOR YOU?

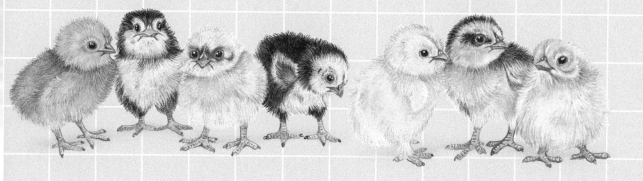

O ften, when people first think of assembling a flock, they focus on aesthetics—how the chickens look and the color of their eggs. While these characteristics can be important, successfully choosing the right breed for your homestead requires a more in-depth approach.

It's all about balancing your goals for your flock with the climate you live in, the temperament you're looking for, and the money you're willing to spend. Maybe you tried raising chickens for eggs in the past, but they didn't thrive. Maybe your grandparents had some chickens that you loved, but you can't remember what breed they were. Maybe you're looking to expand your flock, but you aren't sure which breeds get along with each other. Or maybe you want to help preserve heritage breeds and need to know which one is best suited to your homestead's climate.

This chapter serves as an introduction to assessing chicken breeds for your needs. It covers the basics of chicken anatomy, the key characteristics used for assessment, the basics for building a flock, and the cost considerations of keeping one.

BASIC CHICKEN ANATOMY

As a chicken lover and enthusiast, you can't fully understand your chickens until you understand how the whole bird works, from beak to feet. Let's take a look at the basic anatomy of a chicken.

FUN CHICKEN FACTS

Did you know . . .

- Female chickens are called hens, and baby female chickens are referred to as pullets.

- Male chickens are called roosters or cocks and baby male chickens are called cockerels.

- Hens can lay eggs without a rooster.

- The color of the egg has nothing to do with the nutritional value of the egg and everything to do with the breed of the chicken.

- You will need a rooster to fertilize eggs if you want to hatch baby chicks.

- Chickens are not vegetarians; they are omnivores.

BEAK

A chicken's beak has many uses, from warding off predators to pecking food. The beak is made of bone and keratin and operates much like a human jaw. The beak grows throughout the chicken's life, but its length is maintained through pecking and foraging.

EYES

Chickens rely a lot on their good eyesight. They have motion-sensing cones, making them very good at detecting even the slightest movement, and each eye can work independently of the other. To protect the eyes, chickens have what's called an eye ring, a bit of skin around the eye that can close when the chicken blinks, similar to an eyelid. They also have a third eyelid, a thin membrane that slides over the eye to protect it from debris.

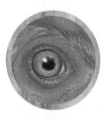

COMB

A comb is located on the top of a chicken's head and has a fleshy rather than feathery texture.

Chicken combs come in many different shapes and sizes, depending on the breed (see page 81). Although typically red, combs can also be purple, brownish, or even black. Blood circulates through a chicken's comb, and it can be an indicator of a chicken's health.

HACKLE

The chicken's hackle is a group of feathers wrapped around its neck. In some breeds, the hackle is the same color as the rest of the feathers, while in other breeds, the hackle is a different color.

WATTLES

Wattles are two folds of skin that hang down on either side of a chicken's beak. While both female and male chickens have wattles, males generally have larger and longer wattles compared with females. As in combs, blood circulates through the wattle, which can be an indication of a chicken's health. Males also use their wattles to attract hens and indicate if there is food close by.

EARS

Although invisible to the human eye, chickens' ears are located on the sides of their face covered by little feathers. They also have small earlobes that look like little folds of skin below their ears. The color of a chicken's earlobes will help you learn what color eggs they lay. A chicken that has white earlobes lays white eggs, while a chicken with colored lobes lays colored eggs.

WINGS

Chickens have two wings that are attached to its breastbone by strong muscles. Although chickens don't fly through the sky like other birds, they are able to fly when all their feathers are grown in, usually in short bursts to escape predators. Some breeds fly better than others. For example, heavier breeds tend to be poor fliers, as their wings aren't strong enough to account for their large mass. This is something to consider if you don't want to clip your chicken's wings.

TAIL

The tail of a chicken is one of its most attractive qualities. You can usually tell the difference between male and female chickens by the tail: Roosters tend to have more impressive tails. Below the tail you'll find the vent, the hole where chickens excrete waste and, in the case of hens, eggs.

FEET

A chicken's legs have scales much like a fish, but a chicken's scales are dry and hard. They have four toes (although some breeds have five), and the male chickens grow spurs. Spurs are made from the same keratin that makes up their beaks. Like our fingernails, spurs grow and need to be trimmed from time to time to help prevent injury to other members of your flock or even yourself.

KEY CHARACTERISTICS AND FACTORS

One of the main goals in choosing a chicken breed is to find the breed that works best for your backyard, homestead, or farm. You want a flock that will suit your needs and complement your lifestyle and environment.

Much like people and other animals, chickens have different character traits. Some traits are generally shared by all chickens, some are breed specific, and some are unique to individual chickens, as nature is unpredictable. Let's take a closer look at common biological, character, and behavioral traits of chickens.

FLIGHT

Most chickens can fly to some extent. However, depending on a chicken's mass-to-wing ratio, some chickens cannot fly very high or for long periods of time. Smaller chicken breeds or those with different body structure possess better flying capabilities. If you live in a neighborhood or don't have high fencing, a breed's ability to fly (or not) may greatly affect your decision.

GROWTH RATE

Every breed of chicken grows to full maturity at a different rate. For instance, some meat chicken breeds grow to harvest weight at as early as nine weeks, while larger chicken breeds may take up to a year or longer to reach their full capacity. If you are looking for chickens to raise for meat for your home or to sell, growth rate will become an important factor.

MOTHERHOOD

If one of your goals is sustainability, you'll want to raise chickens that can multiply. You'll need a rooster as well as hens, and you'll want hens that tend to go *broody*, meaning they like to lay on eggs, hatch them out, and be good mothers.

LIFE EXPECTANCY

When chickens are bred for specific purposes, such as high egg production or fast growth rate, their life expectancy can be greatly reduced. For instance, a Cornish Cross (see page 57) reaches full weight by nine weeks old. If these chickens live past their harvest age (which is nine weeks for Cornish Cross), they experience health issues and die.

EGG PRODUCTION AND COLOR

All chickens lay eggs, but their level of production can vary greatly. Some chickens lay as few as 40 eggs per year, while egg-laying superstars lay over 300 per year! Different breeds of chickens produce different-colored eggshells. It's a common myth that the shell's color is somehow related to the taste and nutritional value of the yolk and white. In reality, color doesn't matter. But your chicken's diet does!

PLUMAGE

When you read, "This chicken has beautiful plumage," it's referring to a chicken's feathers, the appearance of which is unique to each breed. Some breeds have long, flowing feathers, while others have short, fluffy feathers. See the illustrated guide on page 116 for visuals of common feather types.

SIZE AND WEIGHT

Different breeds are different sizes. Some breeds may weigh less than a pound at maturity, and others can be three feet tall. Knowing the standard size and weight for the breeds you are interested in is an important part of the decision-making process.

TEMPERAMENT

A chicken's temperament varies from calm and docile to aggressive. Of course, there are always exceptions to the rule. You can own a breed that is considered to be docile by all standards, and one of your chickens may be mean as a rattlesnake. Understanding the general temperament of the breed—and that Mother Nature may have other plans—is an important lesson for anyone who owns chickens.

CLIMATE HARDINESS

Hardiness is the chicken's ability to withstand its environment and surroundings. If a breed is hardy, it can adapt to changes in its climate, and it tends to have a good immune system. Some chickens are better suited to cold climates, and some are better suited to warm climates. No matter where you live, you'll want to choose a breed that can thrive in your climate.

THE COST OF KEEPING A CHICKEN BREED

Before committing to livestock, it's a good idea to consider cost to make sure you'll be able to afford the upkeep. I made the mistake of forgoing cost analysis when I decided to raise hogs. Little did I know that their feed would be my biggest monthly expense and I wouldn't see a return on my investment for a whole year! For an entire year my pigs were just very expensive, stinky pets.

Fortunately, the cost of raising chickens is a lot more affordable, and they smell better.

For the sake of argument, we're going to pretend that the following costs are the same in every state. Of course, there will always be variables that will affect the cost, but this overview will be a good base point to give you some idea.

BUILDING YOUR COOP

Depending on your construction skill level, the available materials, and how big you need the coop, an average chicken coop will cost between $350 and $1,000. Once your initial investment is made, you will incur little cost thereafter. There will be upkeep costs, such as the cost of fresh bedding, which will run between $7 and $15 a month.

THE BEST-FIT QUESTIONNAIRE

To help you understand some of your needs as you move through this book, think about some of these basic questions. Your answers will help you choose the breeds that will make up your flock.

☐ What is your climate? How cold does it get? How hot does it get?

_____

☐ Why do you want to raise chickens? (Circle your answers.)

Eggs	Pest Management	Pets
Meat		Multiple purposes
Resale	Show	

☐ How much space do you have?_____

☐ Do you want to hatch baby chickens?_____

☐ Do you want roosters and hens?_____

☐ What color eggs do you want?_____

☐ Do you want a specific color of chicken?_____

☐ Do you have children who will be interacting with your

chickens?_____

☐ What other livestock do you have?_____

_____

☐ How big is your chicken coop? _____

☐ What other animals do you have that will be around the

chickens?_____

CHICKENS

Baby chicks are cheaper to purchase than adult laying hens. Depending on the breed of chicken you are buying, the cost range tends to be between $2 and $30 each. If you're looking for more exotic breeds, such as the Ayam Cemani (see page 117), they can cost up to $1,000 each!

If you want to raise chickens and need a rooster, you will only need to make the onetime investment of buying chicks and let nature do the rest. If you don't want a rooster and want more hens, you must purchase chicks/chickens from a hatchery or breeder.

FEED AND TREATS

Baby chickens require a different feed than adult chickens. Some consider adult chickens to be any chicken older than a year old, while others consider them adults when they start laying eggs. I have always switched our chicks over to layer feed when they begin laying eggs, which could be at as early as 16 to 24 weeks. However, this is a personal preference.

0 to 20 weeks of age: Regular grower feed is around $16 for a 50-pound bag. Organic grower feed is around $30 for a 35-pound bag. Layer chicks eat about 20 pounds of feed per chicken for the first 20 weeks. Meat chicks eat roughly eight pounds of feed the first six weeks.

20 weeks and older: Regular layer feed is around $13 for a 50-pound bag. Organic layer feed is around $28 for a 35-pound bag. An adult chicken will eat roughly 1.5 pounds of feed per bird per week.

Treats: Treats are the easy part of raising chickens. They love bugs like worms, crickets, and ticks. They also love food scraps. Every time I make a salad or have leftover pasta noodles, the flock all line up for a treat.

VETERINARY AND HEALTH BILLS

Finding a local vet who treats chickens is like finding the golden ticket in a chocolate bar. Vets who treat chickens are easier to access in rural areas than urban areas. I do have a well-stocked medical kit for our chickens that costs around $60. The cost of veterinary care depends on where you live. In my area, a visit costs around $85 plus the cost of care.

VACCINES

If you order your chicks from a hatchery, they will offer you the opportunity to have them vaccinated. The charge is typically $10 or more per order no matter how many chicks you order. The standard vaccine offered prevents Marek's disease, which is a herpesvirus infection common in flocks. Small backyard flocks don't generally need a lot of vaccinations unless disease has been a problem in the past or they are exposed to other animals, such as at fairs and shows.

CLEANING PRODUCTS

A healthy coop only needs to be deep cleaned once or twice a year. An exception would be if you have a sick bird, in which case you need to clean and sanitize everything. To clean my coop, I use only cleaning vinegar, which costs about $10 per gallon and can be found at most feed supply stores.

SUPPLIES AND OTHER EXPENSES

Bedding: If you are planning to use wood shavings in your coop like I do, the cost is roughly $7 to $15 a month. Another bedding option is sand, which costs around $5 per 50 pounds.

Feeders and waterers: Feeders cost around $16 and last for years. Waterers run from $15 to $30 and will last for years as well. One large feeder should be enough for up to 50 chickens, and a small feeder should be enough for five chickens or fewer. One large waterer should work for about 20 chickens.

Hatching eggs: If you want to hatch your own fertile eggs, you'll need a chicken incubator, which costs anywhere from $60 to several hundred dollars depending on how many eggs you want to hatch at one time.

CHAPTER 2
BEST
PUREBREDS

SUSSEX;
PAGE 20

s you've learned already, there are hundreds of chicken breeds in the world. Domesticated chickens can be subdivided into three broad categories—purebreds, hybrid breeds, and bantam breeds—based on their shared characteristics. This chapter focuses on purebred chickens. We'll learn about the differences between heritage and landrace breeds as well as purebred standards and clubs. And, of course, I'll share my list of the best purebreds for you to consider for your flock.

WHAT IS A PUREBRED?

Think of purebred chickens the way you would purebred dogs. Over the years, they were created by the careful selection of breeders or through natural selection. These breeds have distinctive characteristics—plumage, size, eggs, and so on. Farmers then carefully preserve the breeds' inherent traits by protecting their chicks' lineage: Both parents need to be from the same breed in order to produce purebred chicks.

Purebreds tend to have interesting names, often deriving from the place where they originated. In general, they tend to be a bit flighty, which helps them escape predators—and sometimes their owners, too! Many purebreds are great egg-layers, and they tend to live a long time to boot.

Purebreds can be further categorized into two groups: heritage breeds and landrace breeds. Let's take a look at what these terms mean.

HERITAGE BREEDS

The terms *heritage breed* and *purebred* tend to be used interchangeably, unless you get serious about lineage. Technically, not all purebreds are considered heritage breeds, but all heritage breeds are considered purebreds. Let me explain.

Heritage breeds are the oldest purebreds, and many modern purebreds have descended from them. Heritage breeds are held to high standards (see Purebred Standards and Clubs, page 13). A growing number of farmers and chicken enthusiasts choose to preserve chicken heritage by raising purebreds such as these. In today's world, modern commercial breeds are often chosen over heritage breeds. Remember, heritage breeds are domesticated, so they depend on a farmer's husbandry for survival. If fewer and fewer people raise them, then fewer and fewer heritage chickens exist. It is one reason why I started raising Rhode Island Reds (see page 19).

LANDRACE BREEDS

Landrace breeds are chickens that, over time, have adopted natural traits that help them perform better in their specific region. Land-race breeds produce offspring that closely resemble their parents and can be easily recognizable.

An example of a landrace is the Swedish Flower Hen that Swedish farmers have raised for around 500 years. Another example of a Swedish landrace chicken is the Hedemora. Over several hundred years, the Hedemora has developed a layer of downy feathers to combat the cold winters. Nature has a way of adapting and overcoming, especially if humans don't meddle.

PUREBRED STANDARDS AND CLUBS

The top association for chicken breeds is the American Poultry Association (APA), which is the oldest livestock organization in the United States and is dedicated to only poultry. It defines and publishes the standards for various purebreds and sponsors poultry shows across the country. It also promotes education and fosters community for those in the poultry industry.

The American Poultry Association began classifying chicken breeds in 1873. In order to preserve purebreds, chickens with this classification must meet strict standards. In order to qualify for a heritage breed status, each chicken must:

* Have parentage or grandparentage from stock that was recognized by the APA prior to the mid-20th century. Its purebred lineage should go back multiple generations, and it must possess the traits characteristic of its breed.

- Live a long and prosperous life in pasture outdoor conditions (considered five to seven years for hens and three to five years for roosters).

- Reproduce naturally without assistance.

- Grow to mature weight at a slow and steady pace, reaching the proper market weight by no less than 16 weeks of age.

In addition to the American Poultry Association, there are a variety of other poultry clubs and organizations that focus on various aspects of the industry, such as education, breed conservation, and business development. Here are a few:

- **American Federation of Aviculture:** This is a national organization dedicated to aviculture, which is the practice of raising wild birds (particularly exotic ones).

- **American Livestock Breeds Conservancy:** This nonprofit organization focuses on preserving, protecting, and promoting rare breeds, also known as "heritage breeds," of livestock and poultry, including chickens.

- **American Pasture Poultry Producers Association:** This membership-based organization is all about pastured poultry, a sustainable agricultural technique in which birds are raised in a pasture rather than indoors. The group helps educate the public about pastured poultry and offers support to pastured poultry farmers.

- **American Bantam Association:** This national organization promotes the breeding of bantam poultry (see page 94), a type of purebred chicken. It publishes bantam breed standards, organizes shows and awards, offers resources to bantam breeders, and more.

- **Heritage Poultry Conservancy:** Some heritage breeds are threatened by extinction, and this organization is dedicated to promoting and preserving these heritage breeds for the future.

Individual breeds also have their own breed clubs and associations, which focus on promoting and preserving a single breed. Some of these organizations are national, and some are international. For example, the Cornish (see page 16) has the International Cornish Breeders Association. There may even be more general poultry clubs specific to your area. For example, in Pennsylvania, there is the Pennsylvania Aviculture Society.

THE ULTIMATE PUREBRED CHICKEN LIST

As I've mentioned, many heritage breeds are endangered, and poultry lovers can protect the legacy of heritage breeds by raising them on their farms and homesteads. This list is for anyone who is interested in embarking on this endeavor. This list highlights my picks for the top 10 breeds in the category. Each breed profile covers its characteristic traits, which will help you decide if it is right for your homestead.

COCHIN

Cochins have inspired generations of people to keep chickens. They are large and have a distinctive, pleasing look, with an abundance of large, fluffy feathers, including on their feet. Reaching a good weight at 15 to 16 weeks, Cochins make good meat birds. However, their stunning plumage makes them perfect for show as well. They tend to be docile and friendly and adapt easily to confinement, making them a great candidate for almost any flock. According to the Livestock Conservancy, their status is "recovering."

Origin: China
Purpose: Eggs, meat, show
Climate: Cold hardy
Temperament: Friendly, docile
Average weight: 8.5 to 12 pounds
Harvest age: 15 to 16 months
Egg color: Brown
Egg size: Medium
Egg production: About 160 per year
Feather color: Buff (orange-yellow), black, blue, brown, white, silver laced, golden laced, barred (alternating pigmented bars)
Comb type: Single

CORNISH

Another large heritage breed, the Cornish was initially bred as a game bird. However, the game trait did not transfer to the offspring, and the result was a beautiful meat breed. The Cornish, named after its place of origin—Cornwall, England—was recognized by the APA in 1894. Unlike most breeds, the male and female Cornish are identical. The Cornish had difficulty in the market until the discovery that young birds, now known as Cornish game hens, could be harvested early with tasty results. According to the Livestock Conservancy, their status is "watch."

Origin: England
Purpose: Meat
Climate: Best in warm climates
Temperament: Docile
Average weight: 8 to 10.5 pounds
Harvest age: 4 to 9 weeks
Egg color: Tinted
Egg production: About 50 to 80 per year
Feather color: Dark, white, white-laced red, buff
Comb type: Pea

CUBALAYA

Introduced to the United States in 1939, this elegant-looking chicken originated in Cuba. Their lavish, long "lobster tails" make them easily recognizable. Their glossy tail feathers flow to the ground and are beautiful to look at. Bred for both eggs and meat, not to mention show, Cubalayas are great foragers and do well in pasture. The roosters do not have spurs, which means there are fewer injuries when establishing dominance. They are relatively slow growers, taking up to three years to reach adulthood. According to the Livestock Conservancy, their status is "threatened."

Origin: Cuba
Purpose: Eggs, meat
Climate: Best in moderate to warm climates, tolerates humidity well

Temperament: Calm but active, can be aggressive toward other birds
Average weight: 4 to 6 pounds
Harvest age: Up to 3 years for full maturity (4 pounds for hens, 6 pounds for roosters)
Egg color: White
Egg size: Medium
Egg production: 125 to 170 per year
Feather color: Black breasted, wheaten (yellow wheat), cinnamon, white (rare), blue-red wheaten
Comb type: Pea

DELAWARE

The Delaware chickens were bred in the 1940s for their meat production and white colors. Their white feathers don't leave any color on the skin once plucked, and they weigh a modest six to eight pounds. They were replaced as the breed of choice for meat chicken in the 1950s by the Cornish Cross. Friendly and good for both hot and cold climates, this heritage breed is a good choice for almost any flock. According to the Livestock Conservancy, their status is "watch."

Origin: United States
Purpose: Eggs, meat
Climate: Tolerates most climates
Temperament: Docile
Average weight: 6.5 to 8.5 pounds
Harvest age: 8 months
Egg color: Brown
Egg size: Large
Egg production: 150 to 200 per year
Feather color: White
Comb type: Single

OLD ENGLISH GAME

One of the oldest game hen breeds on record, the Old English Game was first introduced to England around the first century CE. Bred for cockfighting until the mid-1800s, they are now desired for show due to their beautiful plumage. They are a muscular chicken with shiny feathers, which make them a perfect candidate for a show bird. Many of their fighting traits have stayed with them over the past thousand years, and they tend to be aggressive. According to the Livestock Conservancy, their status is "threatened."

Origin: England
Purpose: Show
Climate: Best in moderate to warm climates
Temperament: Active
Average weight: 4 to 5 pounds
Egg color: White to light brown
Egg production: About 120 per year
Feather color: Black, white, spangled (black and white in a V shape), brown red, golden, black-breasted red, brassy
Comb type: Single

PLYMOUTH ROCK

One of the more recognized breeds because of its distinctive pattern of black and white feathers is the Barred Plymouth Rock. Plymouth Rocks are one of the oldest American heritage breeds and were recognized by the APA in 1874. They are sought after for their egg and meat production, second only to Rhode Island Reds, and tend to be calm, hardy, and broody. They often make great additions to a flock. According to the Livestock Conservancy, their status is "recovering."

Origin: United States
Purpose: Eggs, meat
Climate: Tolerates most climates
Temperament: Docile
Average weight: 7.5 to 9.5 pounds
Harvest age: 8 to 12 weeks
Egg color: Brown
Egg size: Large
Egg production: About 200 per year
Feather color: Barred, white, buff, silver penciled, partridge (reddish with black stenciling), Columbian (white with black pattern), blue
Comb type: Single

RHODE ISLAND RED

Rhode Island Reds originated in Rhode Island; they are the state bird and probably one of the United States' best-known breeds. The Rhode Island Red was recognized as a pure chicken breed in 1904 by the *American Standard of Perfection*. It is a great all-purpose bird: a good egg-layer, it is also a hefty meat bird that reproduces well in natural environments. As a heritage breed, Rhode Island Reds are still showing on the cusp of being endangered. According to the Livestock Conservancy, their status is "watch."

Origin: United States
Purpose: Eggs, meat
Climate: Tolerates most climates
Temperament: Docile
Average weight: 6.5 to 8.5 pounds
Harvest age: 4 to 5 months
Egg color: Brown
Egg size: Large
Egg production: 200 to 300 per year
Feather color: Light rust to dark maroon or black
Comb type: Single, rose

SPANISH

Introduced to the APA in 1884, the Spanish chicken is thought to be the oldest breed in the Mediterranean. Its long, dark, green-black feathers; white face; and large white earlobes give this heritage breed a distinctive look. Its face is said to resemble a clown face. Breeding throughout the years to capitalize on this unique feature has been detrimental to the breed's durability and hardiness. According to the Livestock Conservancy, their status is "critical."

Origin: Spain
Purpose: Eggs
Climate: Best in moderate to warm climates
Temperament: Active
Average weight: 6.5 to 8 pounds
Egg color: Chalk white
Egg size: Large

Egg production: About 180 per year
Feather color: Green black
Comb type: Single, rose

SUSSEX

The Sussex breed has been in production since 43 CE. First recognized by the APA in 1914, the Sussex is a great dual-purpose bird and can thrive in a variety of climates. They are a top choice for small homesteads. Their speckled plumage provides them with a natural camouflage to disguise them from predators. According to the Livestock Conservancy, their status is "recovering."

Origin: England
Purpose: Eggs, meat
Climate: Tolerates most climates
Temperament: Docile
Average weight: 7 to 9 pounds
Harvest age: 12 to 16 weeks
Egg color: Tan to brown
Egg size: Large
Egg production: About 200 per year
Feather color: Speckled, light, brown, buff, red, silver, white
Comb type: Single

WHERE CAN I GET PUREBRED CHICKENS?

When I first began raising chickens, I lived in a city without a farm nearby, so I purchased my heritage breeds online from a chicken hatchery. Hatcheries offer a wide variety of chickens and other fowl that can be shipped right to you. You can also contact one of the chicken associations or clubs (see page 13), which offer lists of breeders and their locations. Another source for purebreds is your local feed store. I have several around where I live now that sell them during "Chick Days" each year. The store associates may also be able to point you toward breeders in your area.

WYANDOTTE

Wyandotte chickens became recognized as a member of the *American Standard of Perfection* in 1883. They are admired for their beautiful plumage. Their feathers look like a piece of artwork, and they are a natural candidate for showing. Originating from New York, they are cold hardy, do well in small areas, and aren't good fliers, so they generally do well in backyard flocks. According to the Livestock Conservancy, their status is "graduated," having been removed from the priority list in 2016.

Origin: United States
Purpose: Eggs, meat, show
Climate: Cold hardy
Temperament: Friendly, calm
Average weight: 6.5 to 8.5 pounds
Harvest age: 16 weeks
Egg color: Light to brown
Egg size: Large
Egg production: About 200 per year
Feather color: Barred, black, blue, blue-laced red, buff, buff laced, Columbian, golden laced, mille fleur (mahogany with black bar tip and white spangles), partridge, red, silver laced, silver penciled, white
Comb type: Rose

CHAPTER 3
BEST HYBRIDS

OLIVE EGGER;
PAGE 27

armers and chicken enthusiasts have tried to improve a breed's efficiency in egg and meat production, hardiness, and even temperament by mating them with other breeds that have desirable qualities. Sometimes, different breeds mate with each other naturally. The result in both cases is called a hybrid breed.

In this chapter, we'll discuss the best hybrid breeds of chickens for your flock. Some of my favorite hybrids have the most stunning plumage and colored eggs. I always make sure I have a breed or two of hybrid chickens to add some diversity. In addition to the best breeds, we'll cover the advantages and disadvantages of crossbreeding.

WHAT IS A HYBRID CHICKEN?

A hybrid chicken is one that has parents of different purebreds, either through human assistance (called "development") or naturally, letting the love match happen on its own. Breeders who work with chicken genetics pick specific breeds with desired traits and breed them with other breeds with desired traits to create a hybrid chicken. For example, a breeder may choose a chicken that lays a lot of eggs and breed it with a chicken that has good muscle mass in the hopes of producing a chicken that is both a good layer and a good meat producer.

Chicken genetics are quite fascinating. Different genes carry different traits, and by careful selection, you can breed your own custom chickens for desired traits, such as plumage and combs. Hybrid chickens tend to have some of the most beautiful and unique plumage. When you combine color traits from both parents, the color options of the offspring are unlimited!

Hybrids are designed to outperform all other breeds. They are designed to grow faster and larger, lay more eggs, or produce more meat. Most breeders had production on the mind when developing hybrids in order to meet supply and demand. As the demand on the chickens increases, so do their nutritional needs. Although many hybrids will be excellent foragers, many will still require extra food and protein due to the physical demands of egg and meat production.

Chickens can remember your face. Chickens can recognize and remember 100 different faces. They can also remember if their encounter was a good or bad experience and gossip about it to the other members of the flock!

Because of their fast growth rate and high egg production, you must help meet your chicken's nutritional needs. Failure to do so could result in reduced egg production, poor egg quality, or chickens that are susceptible to sickness and disease.

THE ULTIMATE HYBRID CHICKEN LIST

Hybrid chickens weren't bred frequently until the 1950s. Before that, every farmer raised purebreds. Initially, the tradition of developing hybrids was to increase egg production, but it has since expanded to other traits.

Hatcheries and farmers generally keep their breeding tricks and trades secret so others can't reproduce the same result. Since the practice of combining different breeds has only been around since the middle of the 20th century, the possibilities of new breeds are endless.

Although hatcheries have tried to keep their breeding tricks a secret, there are some hybrids that are available and more common across the nation. In this list, I wanted to share which hybrid breeds have demonstrated vigor and shined in specific categories to make them the best choice for your flock.

BLACK COPPER MARAN

Black Copper Marans are known for their quality of egg over their quantity of egg. Laying a rich, dark brown egg that surpasses all others, Marans are sought after just for their eggs. If you are raising chickens in a colder climate, you will have to give special care to their large combs, as they are susceptible to frost damage. Their appearance is quite pretty, with contrasting black and copper feathers.

Origin: Copper Maran crossed with a Barred
Plymouth Rock
Purpose: Eggs, meat
Climate: Cold hardy
Temperament: Active and docile
Average weight: 7 to 8.5 pounds

Harvest age: 4 to 6 months
Egg color: Dark, chocolate brown
Egg size: Medium large
Egg production: 150 to 200 per year
Feather color: Black with copper on neck and chest
Comb type: Single

BLACK STAR

This breed was created after World War II to be an egg-laying machine in order to aid with the era's food shortages. Black Stars are hardy birds, good foragers, and friendly, making them a great addition to a backyard flock. Although they were bred for egg production, they top out at 8 pounds, so they can be raised as a dual-purpose chicken. Both male and female chickens tend to be striking in appearance.

Origin: Rhode Island rooster crossed with Barred Rock Hen
Purpose: Eggs
Climate: Tolerates even extreme climates
Temperament: Docile
Average weight: 5 to 8 pounds
Egg color: Brown
Egg size: Large
Egg production: About 250 per year
Feather color: Males are black with a white spot on top of their head, and females are solid black. Black pullets (baby female chickens), feather out black with some red feathers in their necks.
Comb type: Single

GINGERNUT RANGER

Gingernut Rangers are very calm, inquisitive birds; make great pets; and can be a good choice for beginners. They are heavy egg-layers as well as meat birds. They are great foragers and will roam the yard looking for food. If you're looking for a good-natured dual-purpose chicken, the Gingernut is the perfect choice.

Origin: Rhode Island Red crossed with a Light Sussex
Purpose: Eggs, meat

Climate: Tolerates most climates
Temperament: Docile
Average weight: 5.5 to 8 pounds
Harvest age: 12 to 16 weeks
Egg color: Brown
Egg size: Large
Egg production: About 300 per year
Feather color: Rich red with either black or white tail feathers
Comb type: Single

GOLDEN COMET

The Golden Comets are at the top of the list when it comes to egg production, which is impressive for their size. They do well in confinement, so they make the perfect addition to a backyard flock. They mature faster than other chickens and start to lay eggs sooner than other breeds, so if you're in a hurry to start collecting eggs, this is the breed for you.

Origin: White Plymouth Rock hen crossed with New Hampshire rooster
Purpose: Eggs
Climate: Cold hardy, heat intolerant
Temperament: Docile
Average weight: 4 to 6 pounds
Egg color: Brown
Egg size: Large
Egg production: About 330 per year
Feather color: Reddish
Comb type: Single

ISA BROWN

ISA Browns are another prolific layer. Laying almost an egg a day, these girls are stars in the coop. They are friendly and love to interact with humans. They adapt to different climates, are good at foraging, and are relatively low maintenance. However, due to their size and egg production, they will need supplemental and additional protein.

> **Chickens are smart.** With a little diligence, chickens can actually be trained. You can teach them to come when called or go into the coop when needed by using treats in conjunction with sound repetition.

Origin: Rhode Island Red crossed with Rhode Island White and a wide range of other undisclosed breeds
Purpose: Eggs
Climate: Tolerates most climates
Temperament: Docile
Average weight: 5 to 6 pounds
Egg color: Brown
Egg size: Large
Egg production: About 300 per year
Feather color: Males are primarily white; hens are tan to copper.
Comb type: Single

OLIVE EGGER

If you're looking to add some diversity to your fresh eggs, an Olive Egger is the chicken for you—as its name suggests, it lays beautiful olive-colored eggs. If you're looking at creating your own hybrids (see the sidebar on page 29), this is one you can make by mating a breed that lays dark-brown eggs with a breed that produces blue eggs, such as the Cream Legbar or Black Ameraucana. It's not a heavy egg producer, but you will love the variety the olive eggs add to your egg basket.

Origin: Cross between a dark-brown-egg-layer and a blue-egg-layer
Purpose: Eggs, meat
Climate: Tolerates most climates
Temperament: Individualized personalities due to genetic diversity; however, Olive Eggers are generally calm
Average weight: 6 to 8 pounds
Harvest age: 16 to 20 weeks
Egg color: Various shades of olive
Egg size: Medium
Egg production: 150 to 200 per year
Feather color: Depends on coloring of parents
Comb type: Varies

PRAIRIE BLUEBELL EGGER

Prairie Bluebell Eggers are rather large chickens with beautiful blue-gray plumage and relatively long legs. Their eggs are blue, and they produce a better-quality egg than other blue egg chickens in their class. They are lightweight and eat less feed than larger birds while maintaining a high egg production.

Origin: Araucana and White Leghorns
Purpose: Eggs, meat
Climate: Tolerates most climates
Temperament: Quiet-natured, docile
Average weight: 5 to 7 pounds
Harvest age: 16 to 20 weeks
Egg color: Blue
Egg size: Medium
Egg production: About 260 per year
Feather color: Dark blue and gray
Comb type: Single

RHODE ROCK

Rhode Rocks have been bred for their egg production and their hardiness. They have great dense plumage that protects them in inclement weather conditions. They are among the heaviest egg-layers, but they also make a decent meat bird. They are great foragers and love to be outside all year round. They can become a bit noisy if they are confined to a small space, so you'll want to keep that in mind if space is an issue for you.

Origin: Rhode Island Red crossed with Plymouth Rock
Purpose: Eggs
Climate: Tolerates most climates
Temperament: Docile
Average weight: 7 to 8 pounds
Egg color: Brown
Egg size: Large
Egg production: About 300 per year
Feather color: Black plumage with gold markings
Comb type: Single

WELSUMMER

The Welsummer breed has been around since the early 1900s and was brought from its home country of the Netherlands to the United States for its large dark-brown eggs. Although it is a hybrid chicken, it is also recognized by the APA. Welsummers are moderate layers, but they are very hardy and great at pest control. They are also generally good-natured and not very good at flying, so they are a good option for backyard homesteads.

Origin: Cross between Rhode Island Reds, Barnevelders, Partridge Leghorns, Cochins, and Wyandottes
Purpose: Eggs, meat
Climate: Tolerates most climates
Temperament: Moderate, docile
Average weight: 4 to 7 pounds
Harvest age: 8 to 9 Weeks
Egg color: Dark brown
Egg size: Large
Egg production: About 180 per year
Feather color: Dark brown with light brown/white feather shafts
Comb type: Single

CAN I CROSSBREED CHICKENS IN MY OWN FLOCK?

If I intrigued you with chicken genetics and you want to be your own mad scientist, you can certainly breed your own hybrid chickens. However, in order to do so, you must have two purebred parents. For instance, in order to produce a Rhode Rock chicken, you must have a purebred Rhode Island Red (see page 19) and a purebred Plymouth Rock (see page 18). Perhaps counterintuitively, you will not be successful in creating true Rhode Rock chickens if you breed two Rhode Rocks together. Dominant traits from one breed or another can show in their offspring, which are not necessarily the same desired traits you see in Rhode Island and Plymouth Rock offspring. You will not get a true hybrid by breeding two hybrids together!

WHITE STAR

White Star chickens were bred to be heavy egg-layers. They produce a whopping 300 to 320 eggs per year! They are a little flighty during youth and prefer to be free range versus raised in a pen, but they tend to calm down and become quite sweet with age. They have a large wattle that can be prone to frostbite, so keep that in mind if you live in a cold climate.

Origin: Considered to be a hybrid chicken that is crossed with four different lines of the old Italian breed White Leghorn
Purpose: Eggs
Climate: Heat tolerant
Temperament: Docile
Average weight: 4 to 6 pounds
Egg color: White
Egg size: Large
Egg production: 300 to 320 eggs per year
Feather color: White
Comb type: Single

CHAPTER 4
BEST BREEDS FOR BEGINNERS

SILKIE BANTAM;
PAGE 37

I was raised with grandparents who had chickens and would sell them and raise them for food. It wasn't until later in life that I decided to raise them myself. I chose to add chickens to our tiny backyard homestead because my family wanted to save on grocery costs, know how our food was raised, and connect with our food source. But knowing what you're in for is important before you invest in your flock. In this chapter, we'll explore the list of the top breeds for beginners.

THE ULTIMATE BEGINNER'S CHICKEN LIST

How long do chickens live? The average lifespan of a chicken is 5 to 10 years (provided they are healthy and don't encounter predators). The Guinness World Records includes a chicken that lived to be 16 years old!

When beginning your chicken-raising experience, you want it to be something that you'll enjoy. Most chickens live between five and 10 years, so even if you don't plan to breed chickens or add to your flock, your first chickens can be a decade-long commitment. I want to start you off on the right foot.

This list highlights the 10 chicken breeds I think are best for beginners, ones that tend to be low-maintenance and good-natured. Of course, there are no guarantees in life. You may choose a chicken breed with a long history of being docile and friendly, but an individual chicken can turn out to be the biggest leg-attacking jerk. On the other side, a breed with aggressive tendencies can turn out individual chickens that are the biggest lap babies you'll ever meet. That is my disclaimer. This list is full of amazing chickens that are perfect for beginners, but there's always that one.

AMERAUCANA

The Ameraucana was developed in the United States in the 1970s and was recognized by the APA in 1984. Ameraucanas are one of the few breeds that lay beautiful blue eggs and are the parent gene of many Easter Eggers. The blue egg gene that chickens have also includes a gene lethal to baby chicks. The Ameraucana was bred to retain the blue egg gene but eliminate the lethal gene. Ameraucanas are good-natured, medium-sized birds that tend to take confinement well. They also do well in cold, though not as well in heat. They are quite stylish, with fluffy earmuffs and beards as well as a pea comb.

Origin: United States
Purpose: Eggs, meat
Climate: Cold hardy, heat tolerant
Temperament: Friendly
Average weight: 5.5 to 6.5 pounds
Harvest age: 22 weeks
Egg color: Blue in various shades
Egg size: Large
Egg production: About 250 per year
Feather color: Black, blue, blue wheaten, brown red, buff, silver, wheaten, white
Comb type: Pea

DORKING

The Dorking is a heritage breed of the landrace descent of England dating back before 43 CE. Originating from an area that takes pride in its high-quality chickens, the Dorking is a top specimen in both meat and egg production. Considered table production birds, they provide great food for the table. Their distinctive features include their five toes and short and stocky build. They don't like to wander from home and will lay eggs in the winter, when other chicken breeds stop. According to the Livestock Conservancy, their status is "watch."

Origin: England
Purpose: Eggs, meat
Climate: Thrives in most climates
Temperament: Docile, friendly
Average weight: 7 to 9 pounds
Harvest age: 16 to 20 weeks
Egg color: White
Egg size: Medium
Egg production: 170 to 190 per year
Feather color: Cuckoo (black and white pattern), dark, red, silver gray, white
Comb type: Single

EASTER EGGER

You don't have to wonder too long how Easter Eggers got their name. They have colorful plumage and lay a wide variety of beautifully colored eggs. Outside of their colored eggs, they also have fluffy cheeks and beards. Sometimes Easter Eggers are mislabeled at hatcheries as Ameraucanas (see page 32), but Ameraucanas are purebreds, and Easter Eggers don't conform to any standard. In fact, hatching Easter Egger eggs is a surprise in every box! They are quite hardy in the cold and tolerant to both heat and confinement. They tend to be friendly, even with children. They are good foragers and will provide you with a steady supply of eggs.

Origin: Cross between a blue egg-layer with a brown egg-layer; typically have one Araucana parent
Purpose: Eggs
Climate: Cold hardy, heat tolerant
Temperament: Friendly, calm
Average weight: 4 to 7 pounds
Egg color: Blue to green and occasionally pink
Egg size: Large
Egg production: 200 to 280 per year
Feather color: Varies widely depending on parentage
Comb type: Pea

FAVEROLLE

During the early 1900s, the Faverolle was the best breed the French produced. Bred for their egg and meat production, Faverolles are visually stunning as well as versatile. They have entertaining personalities and are very inquisitive, although they can sometimes be so submissive that they fall to the bottom of the pecking order in some flocks. They are bred for hardiness and winter egg-laying. As most chickens stop laying in winter, this is the perfect breed to add to your flock so you can have eggs all year long.

Origin: France
Purpose: Eggs, meat
Climate: Cold hardy, heat tolerant
Temperament: Docile, active

Average weight: 6.5 to 8 pounds
Harvest age: 16 to 20 weeks
Egg color: Light brown to pinkish
Egg size: Medium
Egg production: 180 to 200 per year
Feather color: Salmon variety seen in hens is mainly brown, cream, and white. Males have black, brown, and straw-colored feathers. Other varieties include white, black, buff, blue, cuckoo, ermine (white with black pattern), blue-laced, and mahogany.
Comb type: Single

LAVENDER ORPINGTON

Orpingtons are very friendly overall. They are a great all-purpose chicken. They make great mamas and go broody, making them sustainable, as they will keep you in fresh supply of baby chicks. They are good egg-layers, and they are of decent size for a meat bird. Lavender Orpingtons are desired by chicken owners for their good disposition and fluffy, silver-blue feathers, and you could probably make a profit by hatching and selling baby chicks. They are also recognized by the APA as a purebred.

Origin: England
Purpose: Eggs, meat, broody
Climate: Cold hardy
Temperament: Docile, calm
Average weight: 6 to 8.5 pounds
Harvest age: 22 weeks
Egg color: Tinted light brown to pink
Egg size: Medium
Egg production: 175 to 200 per year
Feather color: Silver blue
Comb type: Single

NEW HAMPSHIRE

Developed in New Hampshire and Massachusetts in the early 1900s, New Hampshires were bred for increased egg production and meat production. Breeders were trying to arrive at a faster-growing and better-producing version of the Rhode Island Red. New Hampshires

Chickens can see in color. Chickens can actually see in four different types of cones: blue, red, green, and ultraviolet. Humans can only see in three cones; this makes a chicken's color vision superior to ours.

share many of the same traits as Reds but outperform them. They were admitted to the APA in 1935. While they are known for being docile and good mothers, they can show aggression toward other chickens and might not be the best match with submissive breeds.

Origin: United States
Purpose: Eggs, meat, broody
Climate: Cold hardy, heat tolerant
Temperament: Docile
Average weight: 6.5 to 8.5 pounds
Harvest age: 12 to 16 weeks
Egg color: Brown
Egg size: Large
Egg production: About 200 per year
Feather color: Medium to light red
Comb type: Single

POLISH

One of the most distinctive features of the Polish chicken is its crown of feathers (crest) that sits on top of its head. Polish chickens are stunning to look at and equally entertaining. Although their exact origin is still unknown, they were widely popular in England in the 1700s and made it to American soil in the 1850s. They are docile but skittish because their crest impairs their vision, which also makes them susceptible to predators. A great show bird and a good layer, the Polish breed is a beautiful addition to any flock.

Origin: Holland, Spain
Purpose: Eggs, show
Climate: Can handle heat and cold but not extremes
Temperament: Docile, gentle
Average weight: 4.5 to 6 pounds
Egg color: White
Egg size: Medium
Egg production: About 200 per year
Feather color: Varieties include golden, silver, white, white-crested blue, black-crested white, white-crested black, buff laced
Comb type: V-shape

SILKIE BANTAM

Silkie Bantams are one of the smallest, most adorable breeds of chickens you'll see. Named for their fluffy plumage and silky texture, Silkie Bantams are tiny and unique. In addition to their fluffy feathers, they also have black skin and bones. They love human interaction and are very affectionate. They are low on the egg production scale but make up for it in cuteness. They need protection from wet weather and don't mind being confined in small places. Silkie Bantams make great show birds and perfect pets.

Origin: China
Purpose: Eggs, pet, show
Climate: Cold hardy, heat tolerant
Temperament: Calm, friendly
Average weight: 1.5 to 3 pounds
Egg color: Cream, tinted
Egg size: Small
Egg production: About 100 per year
Feather color: Black, blue, buff, gray, partridge, white
Comb type: Walnut

SPECKLEDY

Speckledy are a hybrid breed from Rhode Island Red and Maran chickens. They mature quickly and produce beautiful dark-brown speckled eggs. Speckledys are extremely friendly and make good pets for those with children. They are heavy, reliable layers (which means they will require more feed than a lighter layer) and enjoy foraging for food.

Origin: United Kingdom
Purpose: Eggs, pet
Climate: Cold hardy, heat tolerant
Temperament: Docile, friendly
Average weight: 3.5 to 5.5 pounds
Egg color: Dark brown, sometimes with specks
Egg size: Large
Egg production: About 270 per year
Feather color: Copper black, copper blue, cuckoo, wheaten
Comb type: Single

WHITE PLYMOUTH ROCK

White Plymouth Rocks are widely known for their calm and friendly personality, which makes them perfect for beginners. They are productive egg-layers all year long, and roosters can be processed at 15 weeks. White Plymouth Rocks are good medium-sized dual-purpose birds that love to forage. They were bred to be good homesteader chickens, so they'll feel right at home in the backyard.

Origin: United States
Purpose: Eggs, meat
Climate: Cold hardy, heat tolerant
Temperament: Docile
Average weight: 7.5 to 9.5 pounds
Harvest age: 15 to 20 weeks
Egg color: Pinkish, medium brown
Egg size: Large
Egg production: 200 to 280 per year
Feather color: Bright white
Comb type: Single

CHAPTER 5
BEST EGG-LAYING CHICKENS

BLACK AUSTRALORP;
PAGE 45

he number one reason most people with backyard flocks start raising chickens is so they can have fresh eggs daily. With the average human consuming around 289 eggs per year, it's no wonder people want to produce their own.

Very few feelings of satisfaction trump that of going to the hen-house and collecting eggs every morning. There is something about raising a chicken, feeding and caring for it, and then collecting the eggs that feed your family that gives you the sensation of empowerment. You know that as long as you have these egg-laying wonders, you'll always have something to eat—even if it's eggs for every meal.

Egg-laying breeds are the most popular chickens. While many are considered dual purpose, the egg-layers are the top of the pecking order, so to speak. This chapter will *eggs-plain* all about eggs and the breeds that are known to be top egg-layers.

ALL ABOUT EGGS

Without getting into the long debate about whether the chicken or egg came first, let's explore the humble egg. Humans have eaten them for thousands of years! They come in different sizes and colors. This section will break all of that down and explain the best ways to store fresh eggs.

WHERE DO EGGS COME FROM?

Only the female chicken can produce eggs. They reach puberty—and gain the ability to lay eggs—between 16 to 24 weeks of age. A hen is born with thousands of tiny ova, the undeveloped yolks, in her ovary, which means she is born with all the eggs she will ever lay in her lifetime. The tiny ova go through a development process, the result of which is an egg. It takes a hen roughly 24 to 26 hours to produce an egg, so a hen will only lay one egg per day at most.

The inside of an egg contains everything that is needed to produce a baby chick, and if fertilized by a rooster, that is eventually what will happen!

A hen requires light to develop eggs, generally up to 14 hours. Therefore, when the days get shorter, a hen's egg production slows down. However, there are some breeds that lay better in winter than other breeds.

A hen does not need a rooster to lay eggs. As a matter of fact, most commercial egg chickens have never met a rooster! You only need a rooster if you want fertile eggs to raise more chickens or a protector for your flock.

EGG ANATOMY

Eggs are a great source of protein and nutrients, including vitamins A, B, D, E, and K as well as calcium, omega-3 fatty acids, potassium, and carotenoids. Different chicken breeds lay different-sized and different-colored eggs, but the anatomy is still the same. Although simple in appearance, the egg of a chicken is complex and marvelous. The eggs contain:

Eggshell: Made of calcium carbonate, the outer shell protects the inside of the egg while letting air and moisture through.

Shell membranes: Made of proteins, the membranes protect the inside of the egg from bacteria.

Chalaza: This twisted little cord connects to the yolk and holds it to the center of the egg.

Albumen: This is the clear part of the egg that turns white when cooked. It's made up of about 40 different proteins and water.

Germinal disk: This is a small circular spot of the yolk. It's where the hen's genetic material is found.

Yolk: The yellow center of the egg. The yolk contains half of the protein content, all the fat, and a major portion of the vitamins of an egg. If the egg was fertilized, the yolk would be the food source for the embryo.

Air cell: This is the air sac inside the egg between the shell and the membrane.

Bloom: This is a protective thin layer on the eggshell.

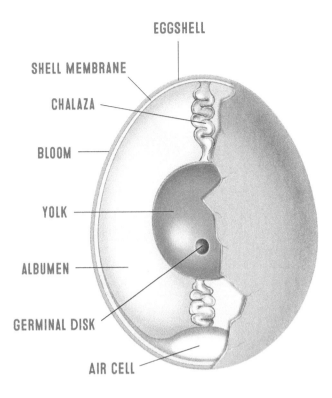

EGGSHELL

SHELL MEMBRANE

CHALAZA

BLOOM

YOLK

ALBUMEN

GERMINAL DISK

AIR CELL

EGG WEIGHT

Eggs come in different sizes and weights. When you shop for eggs in a store, they are usually advertised by sizes, such as medium, large, and extra-large or jumbo. There is a standard by which all eggs are ranked by the USDA, separated, and marketed. Eggs are sorted by grade and size. An egg is judged by three grades: AA, A, and B; AA is the largest, and B is the smallest. There are no nutritional differences in the eggs; the grading system refers only to the size of the eggs and shells.

Eggs sold commercially must be sized and graded. Eggs with a B ranking go to liquid eggs, ingredients, and so on. Grades with an A and AA ranking are weighed and separated by the USDA for retail sale. Farm sales may not have to be graded, depending on state laws, which vary from state to state.

Most recipes that call for eggs use large eggs. Here's a breakdown of the sizes:

Jumbo: 30 ounces per dozen

Extra-large: 27 ounces per dozen

Large: 24 ounces per dozen

Medium: 21 ounces per dozen

Small: 18 ounces per dozen

Peewee: 15 ounces per dozen

EGG COLOR

Believe it or not, the color of the shell has nothing to do with its nutritional value. Even though we've been sold the fact that brown eggs are healthier, that's just a genius marketing ploy to sell brown eggs.

A chicken's genetics determine the color of the shell. A chicken's *diet* and *health* determine the nutrition of what's inside the shell. Eggs of chickens with healthy diets will have a rich, yellow yolk, almost orange in color, and they will taste like eggs should taste— not the pale-yellow yolks that taste like water that you often find in stores.

As I mentioned earlier, eggshells are made of calcium carbonate. Pigments are laid on top of the shell to change its color, or they're added to permeate the shell, depending on the breed of chicken. Although there are no nutritional differences when it comes to shell color, many chicken keepers like to add different breeds to their flocks that provide a rainbow of eggs. No need to dye them for Easter when the chickens can do all the work! Here's an overview of different egg colors:

White eggs: All eggs start out white in color. Colored eggs are caused by pigments that are added from a chicken.

Brown eggs: Brown eggs are caused by pigments that are deposited on the outside of the shell that do not permeate it.

Blue eggs: Blue eggs are caused by bilirubin, and the color permeates the shell.

Other colors: Green, olive, pink, and various shades of brown and blue are formed when chickens with white, brown, or blue eggs crossbreed with one another (see What Is a Hybrid Chicken?, page 23).

EGG HANDLING

Eggshells have more than 17,000 tiny pores on the outside. The bloom that covers the egg as it passes through the oviduct helps protect the egg from outside bacteria. When eggs are washed, like the USDA requires for commercially sold eggs, the bloom is removed, thus making them susceptible to outside pathogens—thus, the need for refrigeration. (For more information, see the sidebar on page 70.)

However, if you keep the bloom intact and store your fresh eggs at room temperature, they will last for several weeks. If you do need to wash your eggs, you will need to store them in the refrigerator. The best advice to keeping your eggs clean is to keep your nesting boxes clean. The cleaner the nesting boxes, the cleaner the eggs.

THE ULTIMATE EGG-LAYING CHICKEN LIST

Egg-layers are the coveted breeds among all chicken owners. A girl that produces a lot of eggs is worth her weight in gold. While all chickens lay eggs and every chicken can be eaten for its meat, my list of ultimate egg-laying chicken breeds contains the cream of the coop in terms of egg production.

AUSTRA WHITE

Austra Whites were developed in the 1900s to replace the Leghorn breed. Like Austra Whites, Leghorns are prolific layers, but they are a hyper breed and skittish. Austra Whites are a calmer breed that produces a lot of eggs. Although they haven't gained the popularity that Leghorns have, they are a great choice for homesteads and make decent meat birds, too.

Origin: Cross between Black Australorp and White Leghorn
Purpose: Eggs, meat

Climate: Thrives in most climates
Temperament: Calm
Average weight: 5.5 to 6.5 pounds
Harvest age: 16 to 25 weeks
Egg color: Cream
Egg size: Large
Egg production: 250-plus per year
Feather color: White with black specks
Comb type: Single

BLACK AUSTRALORP

Black Australorps were bred in the early 1900s by mating a Black
Orpington and a Rhode Island Red. They were designed for egg
production without sacrificing meat production. As egg-layers,
they produce almost all year. In general, they are well suited to
backyard environments.

Origin: Australia
Purpose: Eggs, meat
Climate: Cold hardy
Temperament: Gentle, docile
Average weight: 6.5 to 8.5 pounds.
Harvest age: 16 to 20 weeks
Egg color: Light brown
Egg size: Large
Egg production: 300-plus per year
Feather color: Black with green and purple hues
Comb type: Single

BUFF ORPINGTON

Developed by William Cook and named after his hometown,
Orpington, the Buff Orpingtons were bred to be a large, more
productive chicken to encourage people to raise chickens again.
Orpingtons are the breed of choice when it comes to backyard
chickens in the United States. They often like to be cuddled and
seek out human attention. They are tolerant of human children
and good mothers to chicks.

Origin: Great Britain
Purpose: Eggs, meat, broody
Climate: Cold hardy, heat tolerant
Temperament: Docile, friendly
Average weight: 7 to 8.5 pounds
Harvest age: 22 weeks
Egg color: Light brown
Egg size: Large
Egg production: 200 to 280 per year
Feather color: Orange, beige
Comb type: Single

DOMINIQUE

Recognized as America's first chicken breed, the Dominique is a heritage breed and one worth preserving. Although this breed shares some of the same colors as the Barred Plymouth Rocks, the Dominique is said to be the original breed, having been raised by settlers on the East Coast in the 1750s. They tend to be calm and friendly and generally low maintenance. According to the Livestock Conservancy, their status is "watch."

Origin: United States
Purpose: Eggs, meat
Climate: Cold hardy, adapts to heat and humidity
Temperament: Calm
Average weight: 5 to 7 pounds
Harvest age: 20 weeks
Egg color: Brown
Egg size: Medium large
Egg production: 230 to 250 per year
Feather color: Black and white stripes
Comb type: Rose

HAMBURG

The Hamburg is a heritage breed that has quite a history, dating all the way back to the fourteenth century. It's said that the first-ever chicken show began with an argument in a Hamburg pub about who had the grandest rooster. The Hamburg is indeed a grand rooster with beautiful plumage, and Hamburgs have been winning

Chickens are born with all the eggs they'll ever lay. If you use light in the coop during the offseason, you will decrease the hens' laying years; however, you will maintain a fresh supply of eggs all year long.

shows ever since. Hamburgs like to roost high and aren't a fan of confinement. They consistently lay every year, and their production doesn't drop as they age like other breeds. According to the Livestock Conservancy, their status is "watch."

Origin: Germany, Holland
Purpose: Eggs, show
Climate: Cold hardy
Temperament: Docile
Average weight: 4 to 5 pounds
Egg color: White glossy
Egg size: Medium
Egg production: 200-plus per year
Feather color: White, black
Comb type: Rose

LEGHORN

The Leghorn is a heritage breed that was introduced to the United States around 1870. Although Leghorns come in different colors, the most iconic variety is white. They are a very productive chicken, adapt easily to their surroundings, and can handle pretty much any climate. They love to forage and scratch for their food. Most of the Leghorns around today are an industrial type. You can get the nonindustrial type from small breeders, and they will be hardy, productive, and beautiful to watch, strutting around your yard. According to the Livestock Conservancy, their status is "recovering."

Origin: Italy
Purpose: Eggs
Climate: Heat tolerant
Temperament: Very active
Average weight: 4.5 to 6 pounds
Egg color: White
Egg size: Large
Egg production: 200 to 300 per year
Feather color: White, buff, black, silver, Columbian, red, light brown, dark brown, black-tailed red
Comb type: Single, rose

LOHMANN BROWN

Lohmann Brown is the most common egg-layer in Europe. These chickens were developed in Germany to be egg-laying machines. Laying an average of 300 or more eggs per year, a flock of these beauties is sure to keep you and all your neighbors in eggs. They tend to be easy to handle, and they do well in confinement, making them a good choice for most homesteads.

Origin: Germany
Purpose: Eggs
Climate: Tolerates all climates
Temperament: Docile, friendly
Average weight: 3.5 to 4.6 pounds
Egg color: Brown
Egg size: Jumbo
Egg production: About 300 per year
Feather color: Caramel brown with white
Comb type: Single

WHICH COLOR EGGS TASTE BETTER?

Do brown eggs taste better than white eggs? What about green eggs? Do they taste funny? I was once told by a customer that our colored eggs were old and they wanted "fresh white eggs." Truth is, an egg is an egg is an egg. The difference in the eggs of chickens is simply their diet. If white egg–laying chickens are fed the same diet as green egg–laying chickens, their eggs will taste exactly the same. (You can read more about what gives an egg its color on page 43.)

What a chicken eats has a large influence on how its eggs taste. If your chickens forage on wild garlic or onions, your eggs will have a garlic-and-onion taste. If you ever have an egg that tastes funny, find out what your chickens have been munching on.

NEW HAMPSHIRE RED

Bred for early feathering and fast growth, the New Hampshire Red is a mix of the Rhode Island Red (see page 19) and the New Hampshire (see page 35). It was developed in 1910 in the United States and recognized by the APA in 1935. New Hampshire Reds are good table birds, and the hens produce well, too, making this bird a great all-around performer. They are also easy to handle and bear confinement well. According to the Livestock Conservancy, their status is "watch."

Origin: United States
Purpose: Eggs, meat
Climate: Cold hardy, heat tolerant
Temperament: Docile
Average weight: 6.5 to 8.5 pounds
Harvest age: 16 to 20 weeks
Egg color: Brown
Egg size: Large
Egg production: About 280 per year
Feather color: Rich chestnut red with buff highlights
Comb type: Single

RED SEX LINK

Sex Link chicks can be easily sexed, as male and females have different coloring. This makes them desirable. Along with their color traits, Sex Links are bred to be hardy, very good layers. They come from two heritage breeds, such as a Rhode Island Red rooster and a Delaware hen, that are carefully selected for their desired traits. Sex Links are very domesticated and do well in confined spaces.

Origin: United States
Purpose: Eggs, meat
Climate: Tolerates all climates
Temperament: Friendly
Average weight: 6.5 to 8.5 pounds
Harvest age: 16 to 20 weeks
Egg color: Brown
Egg size: Large

Egg production: 300 per year
Feather color: Medium red to light red
Comb type: Single

RHODE ISLAND WHITE

Rhode Island White chickens were bred in the early 1900s with hopes that the breed would become just as popular as the Rhode Island Red (see page 19). Although they never gained the star status Reds did, they are a wonderful purebred to add to your backyard flock. They lay throughout the winter, when other breeds slow down, and are extremely friendly. They are white all over and have deep, well-rounded breasts—a good choice for a meat chicken as well. According to the Livestock Conservancy, their status is "threatened."

Origin: United States
Purpose: Eggs, meat
Climate: Cold hardy
Temperament: Calm, friendly
Average weight: 6.5 to 8.5 pounds.
Harvest age: 12 to 16 weeks
Egg color: Brown
Egg size: Large
Egg production: 280
Feather color: White
Comb type: Rose

CHAPTER 6
BEST MEAT CHICKENS

JERSEY GIANT;
PAGE 59

Chickens are one of the few livestock that allow people who live in urban areas or who don't own a farm to raise their own meat. There is a growing desire for people to become more connected with their food source so they know what's in their food. From preservatives to added hormones, store-bought meat is looking less like food and more like a science experiment. When you raise your own meat, you know what it ate, you know how it was cared for, and you are part of the process.

This chapter will help you find birds to specifically raise for meat—also called broilers—decide which ones are best for you and your homestead, and provide tips on how to raise them. But first, let's talk about the butcher cuts of a chicken. When you raise chickens for meat, you'll want to make sure you are familiar with and use the whole bird!

POPULAR BUTCHER CUTS

Ever wonder why people always say something tastes like chicken? Chicken has become one of the most widely consumed proteins in the United States. It can adapt to most protein-based recipes, and it can be cooked in a variety of ways. According to the USDA, the average American consumes a whopping 95 pounds of chicken per year! Going by these statistics and the average weight of a meat chicken, one could raise 10 to 11 meat chickens per person in the household each year to satisfy this level of consumption.

You'll hear two terms when it comes to raising meat: market weight and harvest weight. Market weight refers to the ideal weight the chickens needs to be to sell at market. This is dependent on the customer purchasing the meat. Harvest weight is the ideal weight to harvest the chicken before the meat gets too tough. The older the chicken, the tougher the meat.

Raising your own meat means you have control over the quality of meat, and you can also customize your cuts of meat. Chickens can be used whole or divided into four different cuts:

- Breast and tenderloins (white meat)

- Thighs (dark meat)

- Wings (white meat)

- Drumsticks (dark meat)

You may be wondering what to do with the other parts when processing chickens. You may not be used to consuming these now, but some can be scrumptious when cooked properly, and other chicken leftovers have other uses. Here are some ideas on how to utilize the whole chicken:

Organ meats, such as liver, heart, and gizzard: Consume by frying or adding to sausage and pate; grind with other chicken meat to make ground chicken (use as you would ground beef or pork); feed to dogs or meat-eating livestock or animals

Feet: Make gelatin to cook with; feed to meat-eating livestock or animals

Feathers: Use for fly-fishing; use to stuff pillows or comforters

Blood and entrails: Use in compost; use as fish bait

Carcass, bones, and head: Use to make chicken broth

Skin: Fry to make snacks similar to pork rinds; render the fat (called "schmaltz") to use in baking or cooking

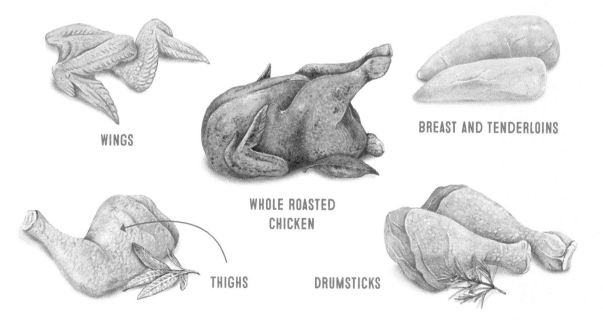

WINGS

WHOLE ROASTED
CHICKEN

BREAST AND TENDERLOINS

THIGHS

DRUMSTICKS

THE ULTIMATE MEAT CHICKEN LIST

This list of meat chickens contains breeds that were bred specifically for meat production. While some are good dual-purpose birds, their main purpose is meat. When raising meat chickens that are designed specifically for meat production, it's important to understand that these breeds are designed to grow big fast. Some breeds will experience health issues if they aren't culled (sent to slaughter) when they are fully grown and will begin to die. You need to be prepared and set up to cull the flock when they are of age. Some breeds live longer than others and will allow you more time.

If you feel that you won't be able to process the birds when needed, consider sticking to dual-purpose meat breeds, which tend to have longer life spans. Keep in mind, too, that due to their fast growth rate and designed purpose, some meat breeds, like the Cornish Cross, are not meant for reproduction. This means you may not be able to use certain birds in breeding programs. Meat chickens also require a higher protein content in their feed than other chickens. When you are raising meat chickens, roosters will tend to weigh more than hens and be larger; however, they taste the same.

With all of that in mind, I've created a list of my all-time top picks for meat chickens. Let's dive in!

BARBEZIEUX

The Barbezieux is considered to be one of the best-tasting meat chicken breeds in the world. Placed against several other meat breeds, the Barbezieux was rated as third-best meat bird by *Gault Millau*, an influential French food guide. The meat is said to have flavor notes similar to those of wild game. If you are interested in the premium meat market, this chicken is for you. These birds are very tall, the tallest breed native to Europe. They almost went extinct in the 1990s, but breeders in Europe rallied to bring them back. If you are looking for something truly unique in your flock, look no further.

Origin: France
Purpose: Eggs, meat

Climate: Thrives in all climates
Temperament: Docile, gentle
Average weight: 7.1 to 9.9 pounds
Harvest age: 18 to 22 weeks
Egg color: White to cream
Egg size: Large
Egg production: About 160 to 200 per year
Feather color: Black feathers with green highlights
Comb type: Single

BRESSE

Noted as one of the best-tasting meat chickens around, the breed has been around for more than 500 years. A true Bresse can only be raised in France, as the name is legally protected (similar to Champagne and other culturally protected products). The ones found in the States are referred to as American Bresse. Their meat-to-bone ratio varies from that of other meat birds, and their genetics allow them to process their food differently, which provides a unique and desirable taste.

Origin: France
Purpose: Eggs, meat
Climate: Cold hardy, heat tolerant
Temperament: Even temperament
Average weight: 6 to 7 pounds.
Harvest age: 4 to 5 months
Egg color: Golden brown
Egg size: Large
Egg production: 250 per year
Feather color: White
Comb type: Single

BUCKEYE

The Buckeye is a heritage breed chicken that is bred as a table chicken, but it can be a good dual-purpose breed, too. Buckeyes' beautiful, thick plumage makes them a good breed for colder climates. They have meaty thighs, have powerful wing and breast muscles, and are a very hardy breed. They have wonderful personalities and love to hunt rodents, giving mice a run for their money. They tend to be very social with humans. According to the Livestock Conservancy, their status is "watch."

Origin: United States
Purpose: Eggs, meat
Climate: Cold hardy, heat tolerant
Temperament: Docile, friendly
Average weight: 6.5 to 9 pounds
Harvest age: 6 months
Egg color: Brown
Egg size: Medium
Egg production: 200 per year
Feather color: Mahogany red with black tails
Comb type: Pea

CHANTECLER

The Chantecler is the first Canadian chicken breed. In the early 1900s, monks set out to create a breed that could withstand the cold climate of Canada and be used for both meat and egg production. It worked: They have a large, meaty breast and can lay in the winter, unlike many birds. If you are looking to build a cold-climate flock, the Chantecler is a clear choice. According to the Livestock Conservancy, their status is "watch."

Origin: Canada
Purpose: Eggs, meat
Climate: Cold hardy
Temperament: Calm, friendly
Average weight: 6.5 to 8.5 pounds
Harvest age: 16 weeks
Egg color: Brown
Egg size: Large
Egg production: 200 per year
Feather color: White, partridge
Comb type: Cushion

COLOR YIELD BROILER

The Color Yield Broiler, a fast-growing meat bird, is a combination of the Cornish Cross and the Red Freedom Ranger. Color Yield Broilers tend to grow a bit slower that the Cornish Cross but faster than the Red Ranger. They are large, heavy, and active chickens. Due to their rapid growth rate, they need extra vitamins so they don't develop health issues as they get closer to harvest weight. You will be shocked how fast these meat birds grow!

Origin: France
Purpose: Meat
Climate: Tolerates all climates
Temperament: Active, calm
Average weight: 8 to 11 pounds
Harvest age: 8 to 10 weeks
Egg color: Brown
Egg production: 175 per year
Feather color: Red, gray, multicolored, white with red flecking
Comb type: Single

CORNISH CROSS

The Cornish Cross is the most popular meat breed and is the one raised by most commercial farmers. It is the fastest-growing breed. Cornish Crosses can reach six pounds by six weeks old, while egg-layers can take up to 22 weeks to reach full weight. Food should be removed from the Cornish Crosses at night to allow their bodies to rest. Otherwise, they could literally eat themselves to death. Cornish Crosses are not meant for breeding or egg production, since they were genetically designed to be raised for meat. Many don't live long enough to reach maturity to lay eggs.

Origin: England
Purpose: Meat
Climate: Does not do well in temperatures above 85 degrees
Temperament: Friendly, roosters can be aggressive
Average weight: 8 to 11 pounds
Harvest age: 4 to 10 weeks (older chickens develop health issues)
Egg color: Light brown

Why does everything taste like chicken? Most store-bought meat is from chickens raised to produce large amounts of meat quickly, never achieving the flavors and taste of wild game. Thus, it absorbs the flavors of what it's cooked with, making everything taste similar.

Egg production: None
Feather color: White
Comb type: Single

FREEDOM RANGERS

Freedom Rangers reach their market weight in just nine to 11 weeks, producing tender, flavorful meat that tends to contain less saturated fat than the meat of other fast-growing breeds. The male Freedom Rangers grow faster than the females and don't have the health problems other meat breeds have. These chickens are hardy and are well suited to the free-range life and foraging.

Origin: France
Purpose: Eggs, meat
Climate: Cold hardy, heat tolerant
Temperament: Calm, friendly, active
Average weight: 5 to 6 pounds
Harvest age: 9 to 11 weeks
Egg color: Light brown
Egg size: Large
Egg production: 125 to 157 per year
Feather color: Red or tricolored
Comb type: Single

WHAT IS THE DIFFERENCE BETWEEN WHITE MEAT AND DARK MEAT?

Chicken breasts, tenders, and wings are white meat, while the legs and thighs are dark meat. The difference, other than color, is that they are two different types of muscles. Dark meat muscles are designed to perform different tasks than white meat muscles. Legs and thighs hold the chicken up and aid in mobility for long periods of time, thus requiring more oxygen and iron. The iron is stored in a protein called myoglobin, which gives the dark meat its color. White meat muscles are designed for short bursts of energy and have the least amount of fat and calories.

JERSEY GIANT

Jersey Giants are the largest purebred chicken in the United States. Due to their size, they require larger living quarters or the ability to free range. However, they aren't as susceptible to predators, such as hawks, as other birds due to their large size. They do take longer to mature than other meat breeds, which makes them perfect for those not in a rush to cull. Jersey Giants are prone to leg breakage. According to the Livestock Conservancy, their status is "watch."

Origin: United States
Purpose: Eggs, meat
Climate: Cold hardy
Temperament: Friendly, docile
Average weight: 11 to 16 pounds
Harvest age: 8 to 9 months
Egg color: Brown
Egg size: Large
Egg production: 150 to 200 per year
Feather color: Black
Comb type: Single

KOSHER KING

Kosher Kings are a hybrid mix of heritage breeds, such as Barred Rock and Sussex. They are similar to a Cornish Cross but grow at a more natural rate, though still faster than a heritage breed. They tend to be quite active birds and do well foraging as free-range chickens. They are not used for egg production.

Origin: United States
Purpose: Meat
Climate: Tolerates all climates
Temperament: Active
Average weight: 6 to 7 pounds
Harvest age: 11 to 12 weeks
Egg color: Brown
Egg production: None
Feather color: Barred, red, silver
Comb type: Single

TURKEN

Is it a turkey, or is it a chicken? Although all chicken, the Turken gets its name from people thinking it was a cross of turkey and chicken, since it has a naked neck like a turkey. (Not coincidentally, Turkens are also called Naked Necks.) They also have 50 percent fewer feathers than other chicken breeds, which makes them easier to clean. Their reduced feathers make them a good breed for warmer climates, but they also tolerate the cold well with proper protection.

Origin: Romania
Purpose: Eggs, meat, broody
Climate: Cold hardy, heat tolerant
Temperament: Docile, friendly
Average weight: 6 to 9 pounds
Harvest age: 6 months
Egg color: Brown
Egg size: Medium
Egg production: About 100 per year
Feather color: Black, white, buff, red
Comb type: Single

CHAPTER 7
BEST EGG AND MEAT CHICKENS

COLUMBIAN WYANDOTTE;
PAGE 66

I 've mentioned dual-purpose chicken breeds a few times in previous chapters. A dual-purpose breed is a chicken that is used for more than one thing, and usually it refers to chickens that are well suited to both egg-laying and meat production. As we've seen, many birds are best suited to one or the other. With dual-purpose breeds, you'll get the best of both worlds.

Keep in mind that you can use almost any chicken for multiple purposes: manure, bug removal, feathers, extra income, and more. But this chapter focuses on those who provide both eggs and meat. We'll take a look at raising dual-purpose chickens, and I'll provide a list of top picks for your flock.

WHAT IS A DUAL-PURPOSE CHICKEN?

Most chickens have been genetically bred (meaning crossbred with other breeds) to excel for a specific purpose. Often, this focuses on either egg or meat production. As we've seen, egg breeds are extremely productive. They can lay 200 or more eggs a year, and because they tend to grow slowly and do not become as well developed, it doesn't make sense to cut their life short and use them for meat.

On the other hand, birds that were bred for meat production can grow extremely fast. Their muscles become well developed, and they tend to have qualities that make them succulent and flavorful when cooked. Because of the fast growth rate, some meat breeds don't have a long enough life span to lay *any* eggs, let alone be productive egg-layers.

Dual-purpose birds have been bred to be productive in both egg and meat production. They are often great options for homestead flocks, since they are multipurpose.

HOW MANY CHICKENS DO YOU NEED?

A good dual-purpose chicken will provide you with a satisfactory amount of eggs as well as a decent meat-to-bone ratio. Many people who raise dual-purpose breeds will cull the excess roosters for meat and keep the hens for laying eggs.

A flock will only need one rooster per eight to 10 hens. Too many roosters in a flock cause fights among the roosters and stress among hens who don't appreciate the extra mating advances. Stressed hens don't lay eggs, which is counterproductive.

Every time an egg hatches, you have a 50/50 chance of it being a rooster. Considering that a chicken can hatch 12 to 15 eggs per clutch—the group of eggs a hen can lay on to hatch—you may end up with a lot of excess roosters. "Extra" roosters that can't be sold are generally raised for meat. Roosters also tend to weigh two to four pounds more than hens, so they provide more meat than their female counterparts.

You can raise enough chickens to provide for all your family's egg and meat consumption. For example, our family of four consumes two dozen eggs per week, and we eat two whole chickens per week. If we wanted to raise all our own eggs and meat and not have to buy any from a store, we would need to raise 104 meat chickens per year and have enough egg-laying hens to produce 1,248 eggs.

Using our breed descriptions, you can choose what dual-purpose breeds will provide for your family's egg and meat consumption. Keep in mind that all the numbers are approximate. Many factors play a role in production, such as weather, housing, predators, nutrition, specific breed, and health.

> Chickens have tast buds. You would think anything that pecks through poop to eat undigested food wouldn't have taste buds, but they do—between 240 and 360 taste buds (a fraction of the 10,000 that humans have).

THE ULTIMATE EGG AND MEAT CHICKEN LIST

Use this information to determine how many chickens you need to supply your family with enough meat and eggs for the year.

AMBER WHITE

Amber Whites were created for their high egg production but also make amazing table birds. They do well with other chicken breeds and in confinement. They are a cross between Rhode Island Whites and Rhode Island Reds. Because of their sweet nature, they make a perfect chicken for beginners, too.

Origin: United States
Purpose: Eggs, meat

Climate: Cold hardy
Temperament: Docile, friendly
Average weight: 5 to 6 pounds
Harvest age: 12 to 16 weeks
Egg color: Yellowish, brownish
Egg size: Large
Egg production: 300 per year
Feather color: Cream with brown specks
Comb type: Single

BIELEFELDER

Bielefelders are a somewhat new breed to the chicken world. Developed in the 1970s from Amrocks, Malines, Rhode Island Reds, and New Hampshires, they are considered an excellent dual-purpose breed for their wonderful egg-laying ability and great meat quality. They are easy to raise and handle as well. Topping out at nine-plus pounds, they make a great table bird.

Origin: Germany
Purpose: Eggs, meat, pet
Climate: Cold hardy
Temperament: Docile, friendly
Average weight: 6.5 to 9-plus pounds
Harvest age: 12 to 16 weeks
Egg color: Brown
Egg size: Large
Egg production: About 230 per year
Feather color: Multicolor: brown, black, cream, white
Comb type: Single

BRAEKEL (BRAKEL)

The Braekel, one of the oldest European breeds, has been around since the early 1400s as a staple household chicken, but it almost went extinct after World War II. During the 1970s, efforts were made to preserve this beautiful breed and increase its population. Braekels have distinctive white-and-black banding with a solid neck color. They are a hardy breed, as they were originally left to fend for themselves, and are also considered disease resistant. They were developed for egg production, but as they mature relatively quickly, they make a good table bird as well.

Origin: Belgium
Purpose: Eggs, meat
Climate: Tolerates all climates
Temperament: Active
Average weight: 4.8 to 5.5 pounds
Harvest age: 14 to 20 weeks
Egg color: White
Egg size: Medium to large
Egg production: 200 per year
Feather color: Silver or gold, solid necks, banded body feathers
Comb type: Single

CINNAMON QUEEN

Cinnamon Queen hens tend to start laying sooner than other breeds. They do well in confinement, which makes them a good choice for backyard flocks. Cinnamon Queens tolerate the cold well and tend to be good mamas, so you always have a supply of chicks. They are heavy layers but also make a good table bird. Like the Sex Links (see page 49), you can identify the males and females at birth. The male chicks are white, while the female chicks are reddish brown. If you're raising chickens for both meat and eggs, you can separate the males to raise for meat production from birth.

Origin: United States
Purpose: Eggs, meat
Climate: Cold hardy
Temperament: Docile, friendly
Average weight: 5.5 to 7.5 pounds
Harvest age: 16 to 18 weeks
Egg color: Brown
Egg size: Large
Egg production: 250 to 300 per year
Feather color: Cinnamon
Comb type: Rose

COLUMBIAN WYANDOTTE

The Wyandotte (see page 21) also appears on the best purebred list, but the focus is on the Columbian Wyandotte here. Wyandottes first made their debut in the United States in 1893 at the World's Fair. People have been raising them ever since. They have beautiful plumage and make good mothers. They do well in confinement and in free range. They are also extremely cold hardy, something to keep in mind if you live in northern climates. They also continue to lay in the winter. According to the Livestock Conservancy, their status is "graduated," having been removed from the priority list in 2016.

Origin: United States
Purpose: Eggs, meat, broody, show
Climate: Cold hardy
Temperament: Docile
Average weight: 6.5 to 8.5 pounds
Harvest age: 16 weeks
Egg color: Light to rich brown
Egg size: Medium large
Egg production: About 180 per year
Feather color: White with black
Comb type: Rose

CROAD LANGSHAN

This heritage breed originated in China, and Croad Langshans are known to have full breasts and rich, flavorful meat. They are also decent egg-layers and quick growers. The males can weigh close to 10 pounds at harvest. They tend to be easy to raise and take to confinement well. Their look is striking, too. Aside from being a relatively tall chicken, their stunning plumage and feathered legs make them a good show breed. According to the Livestock Conservancy, their status is "watch."

Origin: China
Purpose: Eggs, meat, show, pet
Climate: Cold hardy, heat tolerant, doesn't do well in wet climates
Temperament: Very calm
Average weight: 7.5 to 9.5 pounds

Harvest age: 16 weeks
Egg color: Dark brown, sometimes with a purple hue
Egg size: Large
Egg production: 150 per year
Feather color: Black, green sheen
Comb type: Single

IXWORTH

The Ixworth breed was named after the town it originated from in England. It was developed as a dual-purpose breed in 1930 for a fast-growing, high-quality meat bird that lays a large amount of eggs. Some say that the Ixworth provides the tastiest meat of any purebred chicken. Ixworths almost went extinct around 1970 but have since recovered thanks to chicken enthusiasts working to preserve the breed.

Origin: England
Purpose: Eggs, meat
Climate: Cold hardy
Temperament: Active, alert
Average weight: 7 to 9 pounds
Harvest age: 8 to 9 months
Egg color: Light brown tint
Egg size: Medium
Egg production: About 270 per year
Feather color: Pure white
Comb type: Pea

MARSH DAISY

Marsh Daisy is one of the United Kingdom's rarest breeds. It was created by breeders in the late 1800s in Lancashire, England, with a bloodline that includes Old English Game Bantam, Cinnamon Malay, Black Hamburg, White Leghorn, Pit Game Cock, and Sicilian Buttercups. This breed was almost extinct and then rediscovered in Somerset in the 1970s. They are great foragers and mothers and well suited to free ranging, notably in wet areas, which legend says is how this bird got its name. This is the perfect breed for the chicken enthusiast.

Chickens may be able to outrun you. Chickens have the amazing ability to run up to 9 mph! If you're planning on chasing a chicken, either bring good running shoes, or have some treats they enjoy.

Origin: United Kingdom
Purpose: Eggs, meat, broody
Climate: Cold hardy, heat tolerant
Temperament: Active, friendly
Average weight: 5 to 7 pounds
Harvest age: 12 to 16 weeks
Egg color: Tinted light brown to pinkish
Egg size: Small to medium
Egg production: About 280 per year
Feather color: Brown, wheaten, buff
Comb type: Rose

MASTER GRAY

The Master Gray is a beautiful specimen that's been around for more than 100 years. Its plumage allows this breed to participate in shows, while its traits make it a good dual-purpose chicken. Its black feathers are muted by its thin white feathers, giving it a gray appearance. Master Grays are good for all climates and are a healthy and hardy breed.

Origin: France
Purpose: Eggs, meat, show
Climate: Prefers warm climate but tolerates cold
Temperament: Active, friendly
Average weight: 8 to 13.5 pounds
Harvest age: 12 to 16 weeks
Egg color: Cream, brown
Egg size: Large
Egg production: 200 to 300 per year
Feather color: White with black
Comb type: Single

CHAPTER 8
BEST BROODING CHICKENS

ASEEL (OR ASIL);
PAGE 76

If one of your goals is sustainability, then you will want to be able to raise your own baby chicks. Creating a constant supply of chickens to meet your needs is the only way to become sustainable in terms of keeping a flock. Your meat chickens will be harvested, and egg-layers will eventually expire, too—and there are always accidents and predators to contend with. Sure, you can order new chicks every spring, but that can become expensive, and you are never guaranteed delivery. Alternatively, you can raise your own chicks. Outside of raising enough chickens for your personal needs, you can also sell chicks or fertile eggs to others to make an income and monetize your homestead.

Not all breeds are well suited to brooding, or the maternal instinct that encourages a hen to sit on her clutch. Likewise, some breeds are more inclined than others to help raise the chicks. This chapter focuses on what it takes to raise chicks and provides a list of the best broody breeds for your flock.

FROM CHICKS TO ADULT CHICKENS

Undeniably, baby chickens are one of the most adorable things you'll ever see. Just ask any child who goes into a feed store during

TO REFRIGERATE OR NOT TO REFRIGERATE?

This may come as a shock to you, but in many other countries, people don't refrigerate their eggs. When a chicken lays an egg, a protective bloom, or cuticle, is added to the egg as it leaves the chicken's body. The eggshell itself is made of calcium carbonate and is very porous. Bacteria can get inside an egg through the shell. However, the bloom prevents this from happening. In the United States, by law you have to wash any eggs you sell; therefore, the protective bloom is removed, making the egg susceptible to bacteria entering through the shell. This makes refrigeration necessary. In other countries, they don't remove the bloom, making refrigeration unnecessary. Many chicken keepers are privy to this information and opt not to wash eggs they will personally consume, so they also feel safe leaving them on the counter until they use them.

"Chick Days." You can hear "Aw!" and "I want one!" all the way through the store.

However, like all animals, chicks are a commitment—of your time and your wallet. When contemplating raising chickens, you must consider their housing, local laws, and breeds as well as the fact that you'll be their caretaker for close to a decade or more. The job isn't something that pairs well with frequent travel, for example.

To start raising chickens, you need two things: a rooster and a broody hen. The term *broody* refers to the maternal instinct of a chicken to raise babies. Just like all other animals, some chickens are natural-born mothers, and some aren't. Raising chicks is easier with a broody hen. On the other hand, some chickens are so good at being mamas they never want to leave the nest—to the point that their health starts to decline because they aren't getting enough food or water.

Keep in mind that there is no breeding cycle for chickens, and some chickens lay eggs all year round. If you have a good rooster-to-chicken ratio (the average is one rooster for 8 to 10 hens), you can assume most of your collected eggs will be fertile. There's no need to separate hens from roosters unless the roosters become too aggressive.

A broody hen is an asset to her flock. She will help hatch and raise baby chicks to keep you in supply of chickens. Additionally, a broody hen won't care what breed of eggs she's laying on, even species. I've seen chickens hatch ducks, turkeys, and guineas. This means that one broody hen can help hatch the eggs of the other, less-broody hens in your flock. An average-size broody hen will lay on 12 to 15 eggs. She needs to be able to cover the eggs with her body to keep them warm.

If you don't have a broody hen, you'll need an incubator to hatch them for you. If you are raising chickens from the chick stage, you will be more hands-on than if the mama hen was hatching her own chicks. After your chickens reach the adult stage, there is less micro-managing that you must do, but it's still a daily commitment. Let's take a look at what you can expect from each stage of development.

FROM EGG TO HATCH DATE

Once a fertile egg has been laid, it takes about 21 days to hatch. The only true way to know if an egg is fertile is to hold a light (like a candle) against the shell to illuminate the inside. You can candle on day 4 to see if the embryo is starting to develop and then again on day 10 and 17 to see how things are progressing. Keep in mind that broody hens generally don't like being messed with, though.

Chicks will start to peck their way out of the egg around the third week of incubation, and begin their cute little chirps.

As tempted as you may be, don't "help" the chicks out of their shells. This is something they need to do on their own. A chick can take up to 24 hours to hatch out of its shell. "Helping" a chick hatch can cause harm if it's still connected to the membrane, causing unintended injuries. It's best to let nature do its thing. A chick that needs help hatching is likely to have health issues and may be weak genetically; it may likely be the runt of the litter.

WEEKS 1 TO 4

This is the cute fluffy baby chick stage. If mama is raising them, you can leave her be and let her instincts do what they do best. If she hatched her chicks in an unsafe location (they tend to do that), then you can carefully move mama and babies to the safety of their coop. (It's even better if she has her own fenced-in run and coop to raise the chicks away from the older, higher-ranked chickens, which may bully her or the new chicks, which start at the bottom of the pecking order.) An unsafe location would be anywhere the chicken doesn't have shelter or protection from predators.

If you notice mama laying on eggs outside her nesting box, you can try to relocate the eggs and the mama to the nesting box in the coop. However, there is a chance that she won't be happy with you doing so and may try to move them again or give up laying on the eggs.

Hens do not feed baby chicks but will lead the baby chicks to food. Regardless, the chicks will need starter chicken feed, which has a different nutrient mix designed for growing birds, and a fresh supply of water daily. Baby female chickens are called pullets, and baby male chickens are called cockerels.

WEEKS 5 TO 16

These weeks are the awkward teen years. Cute little baby chicks start to grow their feathers and look a little funny in the process. They start to want to roost, develop their personalities, and establish pecking order.

Their combs start to develop as well as some of their gender differences. They still need to be fed starter and grower feed until they are old enough to lay eggs, which is typically between 16 and

RHODE ISLAND RED

Weeks 1–4   Weeks 5–16   Weeks 17–22   Week 22 and after

BUFF ORPINGTON

Weeks 1–4   Weeks 5–16   Weeks 17–22   Week 22 and after

BARRED PLYMOUTH ROCK

Weeks 1–4   Weeks 5–16   Weeks 17–22   Week 22 and after

22 weeks. You can transition roosters to regular chicken feed at this time, too. When chicks grow in all their feathers and get bigger, they are ready to introduce to the rest of the flock.

WEEKS 17 TO 22

Now is the time when your hens start to lay eggs, and you wait for the coveted egg song. It is like no other noise your hens will make. Much like a rooster's crow, the egg song is specific to the hen that is laying the egg. I can always tell when one of our girls is laying by what noise she is making. As for the roosters, they will start to crow around this time, and you'll begin to notice a lot of breeding.

When your hens start laying eggs, you'll want to switch them to a layer feed. Some breeds lay sooner than others, and other factors, such as weather, can play a role in timing. Sometimes, you'll just need to be patient!

WEEK 22 AND AFTER

Now that your chickens are all adults and you're getting fresh eggs daily, it's time for them to molt. Chickens molt much like other animals get a winter coat and shed. The feathers on a chicken provide them with protection from the elements. Over time feathers break and lose their natural oils, so chickens molt in order to produce new feathers. You will begin to see feathers all over the bottom of the coop floor, and egg production will slow down if not stop altogether. Don't worry: The new feathers will fill in just fine, and eggs will start showing up again before you know it.

ONE YEAR AND AFTER

If you've raised your hens with roosters, chances are a large portion of your eggs are fertile. It's perfectly fine to eat the ones you don't plan to raise. In fact, if you are collecting eggs every day or so, there is really no way to tell whether an egg is fertilized. Fertilized eggs need to be kept at a very specific temperature to remain viable, so once you remove them from the nest, the embryo stops developing.

Keep in mind that you may not have any broody hens during the first year, so if you want to hatch baby chicks, you'll need to invest in an incubator. Generally, hens will produce the largest amount of eggs during their first year of life and reduce production in subsequent years. However, some breeds are consistent layers throughout their entire production cycle.

ONCE A HEN STOPS LAYING

Remember, a hen is born with all the eggs she will ever lay, so the day will come when she stops laying altogether. A hen needs 12–14 hours of light per day to produce an egg. As the days get shorter, egg production slows down, which allows the chickens to rest. This extends the chickens' egg production years because they are taking breaks from laying throughout the year and not producing eggs daily. If an artificial light is used in the coop to stimulate continuous egg production, a hen will have fewer production years than if no light is used.

So how many years will she produce? Let's say your chicken was born with 600 eggs in her reproductive system, and she lays 200 eggs per year. You can then expect your chicken to lay eggs for three years of her life. However, if you use a light in the coop and that chicken is now laying 300 eggs a year instead of her normal 200, she will lay eggs for only two years instead of three.

Most breeds reliably lay eggs for two to three years. After that, production starts to decline. When a hen stops laying eggs, you have one of three choices:

1. If she is known for going broody, you can use her to hatch out eggs for you. A broody hen will sit on fertilized eggs even if she has stopped producing them herself.

2. Cull her for meat consumption.

3. Let her live out her golden years on the homestead until she quietly passes.

At the end of a hen's production years as an egg-layer, you can make the best choice for you and your homestead. If the preceding choices are not viable options to you, there are many people who would love to adopt a good hen just as a companion.

THE ULTIMATE BROODING CHICKEN LIST

A broody hen is essential to a self-sufficient homestead. She is the one that will hatch and raise future generations. As I've mentioned, not all hens are good mamas or like to sit on eggs for 21 days. If you get a good broody hen in your flock, take special care of her, because she will hatch out not only her eggs but also the eggs of other chickens and other fowl, as well.

Keep in mind, too, that there are always exceptions to every rule. Although the breeds mentioned here are known for going broody, that doesn't mean it's written in stone and that every individual will.

ASEEL (OR ASIL)

Originating in India, the Aseel is probably the world's oldest game fowl breed. This heritage breed is very muscular and has an innate instinct for survival. The hens make excellent mothers and will protect their young at all cost. They are known for being tenacious and intelligent. They do better on free range rather than in confinement. According to the Livestock Conservancy, their status is "threatened."

Origin: India
Purpose: Meat, broody, show
Climate: Cold hardy, prefers dry environment
Temperament: Aggressive
Average weight: 4 to 5.5 pounds
Harvest age: 6 to 8 months
Egg color: Cream
Egg size: Small
Egg production: About 40 per year
Feather color: Black-breasted red (wheaten), dark, spangled, white; game colors, such as gray, blue-breasted red, and black. Many color variations have a metallic luster or sheen and can look green or purple depending on the light.
Comb type: Pea

BELGIAN BEARDED D'UCCLE

This tiny little feathered wonder is not only a great mother but also a wonderful pet. The hens love to go broody and will even hatch a full-size egg despite being so small themselves. However, their small build limits the number of eggs they can hatch. Originally from France, these birds come in a diverse array of colors and have feathered legs.

Origin: France
Purpose: Broody, show, pet
Climate: Cold intolerant, heat tolerant
Temperament: Docile, calm, friendly
Average weight: 1 to 1.5 pounds
Egg color: Cream or tinted light pink
Egg size: Small
Egg production: 100 per year
Feather color: Mille fleur, black, porcelain (beige or straw), golden neck, mottled (marked with spots), self-blue (lavender), white
Comb type: Single

BUFF COCHIN BANTAM

The Buff Cochin Bantams are the mini version of the Cochins (see page 15) and also have feathered feet. They make great pets and even better mothers. They love to sit on eggs and go broody. They were brought in from China in the mid-1800s and are still a top show bird.

Origin: China
Purpose: Broody, show, pet
Climate: Cold hardy
Temperament: Docile, friendly
Average weight: 26 to 30 ounces
Egg color: Light brown
Egg size: Small
Egg production: 100 to 160 per year
Feather color: Buff
Comb type: Single

CUCKOO MARANS

Cuckoo Marans look much like the Barred Plymouth Rock (see page 105) but lay lovely dark-brown eggs, a trait that many covet. They were developed in France in the early 1800s. They are hardy birds that bear confinement well. They also like to go broody and make excellent mothers.

Origin: France
Purpose: Eggs, meat, broody
Climate: Cold hardy, heat intolerant
Temperament: Friendly
Average weight: 7 to 8.5 pounds
Harvest age: 16 to 20 weeks
Egg color: Dark chocolate color
Egg size: Large
Egg production: 150 per year
Feather color: Dark feathers barred with irregular dark and light slate-colored bars
Comb type: Single

SPECIAL DIETS FOR BROODY HENS

All mothers need special care, and chickens are no exception. Some broody hens are extremely dedicated and refuse to leave their nest. This can harm a hen's health, and it's important to pay special attention when you have a broody hen to make sure she is eating and drinking properly. Make sure to offer her food and water close to her nest so she doesn't have to travel far. You may even place a small dish in her nesting box. A comb that is fading in color can be a sign that she's not receiving enough nutrition. If this happens, you can remove her from the nesting box for a little bit of time each day to ensure that she's getting some sun and food. Offer her extra calcium, such as yogurt or crushed oyster shells, as well as cooked oatmeal and worms.

EGYPTIAN FAYOUMI

Fayoumi are an exotic breed of chicken that is said to have developed in Egypt from an ancient jungle fowl. They tend to be quite independent and are excellent at foraging and scanning for predators in the yard. These chickens mature quicker than most other breeds and do well as broody mothers and meat birds. They lay around 150 eggs per year, which is better than other broody hens, and they are the perfect roaster size.

Origin: Egypt
Purpose: Meat, broody, show
Climate: Cold intolerant, heat tolerant
Temperament: Flighty and active
Average weight: 3.5 to 5 pounds
Harvest age: 16 to 20 weeks
Egg color: Cream
Egg production: 150 per year
Feather color: Silver and white
Comb type: Single

ICELANDIC

Icelandics are long-lived, hardy, and great foragers. They have strong mothering instincts and tend to go broody often. They are a landrace heritage breed bred to survive the Icelandic climate and survive on their own as foragers. They do not do well in confinement. Icelandics provide meat, eggs, and the ability to raise chicks. According to the Livestock Conservancy, their status is "threatened."

Origin: Iceland
Purpose: Eggs, meat, broody
Climate: Cold hardy, heat tolerant
Temperament: Friendly
Average weight: 3 to 5.5 pounds
Harvest age: 16 to 20 weeks
Egg color: White to light cream
Egg size: Medium to large
Egg production: 180 per year

Feather color: Not standardized in appearance
Comb type: Single and rose

JAPANESE BANTAM

This tiny historic breed is said to have originated before the 1600s from China. It is a true bantam, which means it was never bred as a standard-size chicken. However, it has a gene that makes a quarter of its eggs unfertile. On the plus side, the hens are great broody mothers, so a three-quarters hatch rate is still good. They do not do well in cold and are prone to frostbite.

Origin: China
Purpose: Broody, show
Climate: Cold intolerant, heat tolerant
Temperament: Calm, docile, friendly
Average weight: 1.1 to 1.3 pounds
Egg color: White to pale brown
Egg production: 80 to 160 per year
Feather color: White, buff, black-tailed buff, black, silver gray, tricolor, wheaten, blue red, brown red, dark gray
Comb type: Single

JAVA

Large hardy birds, the Java are one of the oldest breeds from the United States. The first record of them is in 1835, but they were around well before then. Although they grow slowly, they were once a premier meat production bird. They do well on free range. They are strongly broody and very protective of their young. Chicken enthusiasts are working to preserve this heritage breed. According to the Livestock Conservancy, their status is "watch."

Origin: United States
Purpose: Eggs, meat, broody
Climate: Tolerates all climates
Temperament: Hardy, calm
Average weight: 6.5 to 8 pounds
Harvest age: 16 to 24 weeks
Egg color: Brown

AN ILLUSTRATED GUIDE TO CHICKEN COMBS

BUTTERCUP

ROSE

WALNUT

SINGLE

V-SHAPED

STRAWBERRY

PEA

CUSHION

Egg size: Large
Egg production: About 150 per year
Feather color: Black (often with metallic, black-green sheen), mottled, white, auburn
Comb type: Single

MODERN GAME

Much like the Aseel (see page 76), the Modern Game hens lack in egg production but make up for it in broodiness. They are very protective and instinctive mothers. They were originally bred for show, and they can be tamed easily and make good pets. However, they don't do well in confinement and tend to be quite active.

Origin: United Kingdom
Purpose: Broody, show, pet
Climate: Cold intolerant, heat tolerant
Temperament: Occasionally aggressive, friendly
Average weight: 6 to 8 pounds
Egg color: White to cream
Egg production: 50 to 80 per year
Feather color: Black red, black brown, pyles (white body with golden head)
Comb type: Single

NANKIN BANTAM

Nankin Bantam is one of the oldest heritage breeds around. Many of the small breeds have a larger counterpart, but the Nankin is a true bantam and doesn't have a larger version.

Origin: United Kingdom
Purpose: Broody, show
Climate: Tolerates all climates
Temperament: Docile
Average weight: 1 to 1.5 pounds
Egg color: Tinted cream
Egg production: 80 to 100 per year
Feather color: Red buff with dark black tail feathers
Comb type: Single or rose

CHAPTER 9
LARGEST CHICKEN BREEDS

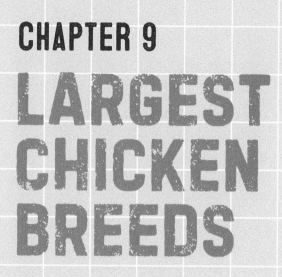

MALINE;
PAGE 90

There are so many different factors to consider in deciding which breeds to get for your homestead, such as temperament, purpose, and the goals you have for the chickens you raise, such as show, pet, or food. There's also size to consider. Do you want a small breed, a large breed, or something in the middle? Small breeds, called bantams (see page 93), are often sought after because they work well in limited yard space, but that is not the only consideration. Small breeds tend to become prey, while large breeds are more intimidating and less apt to have a predator swoop out of the sky and haul them away.

Large-breed chickens are often referred to as gentle giants. They are large in stature, some more than three feet tall and most weighing between eight and 15 pounds. They make great pets as well as dual-purpose livestock. In this chapter, we'll explore the pros and cons of owning large breeds, and I'll share my list of top large-breed chickens for your flock.

PROS AND CONS OF LARGE CHICKENS

As with any breed, there are always pros and cons. When you choose large-breed chickens, there are some things you'll have to take into consideration. Let's take a look at each.

PROS OF LARGE CHICKEN BREEDS

Less prone to predators: If you live in a predator-prone area, fencing alone doesn't always protect your flock. I've seen bobcats and foxes pull chickens right through a fence before! Large chicken breeds make that task more daunting for would-be predators.

Less fragile: Chickens are delicate little creatures by nature. For example, sometimes a loud noise can actually scare a chicken to death. The larger breeds, however, aren't as fragile as smaller breeds.

Make great show birds: Who doesn't want to see a chicken the size of a full-grown turkey? Many large chicken breeds make great show chickens simply for their size—not to mention their beautiful plumage and unique features such as enormous legs.

More meat: If you want to raise chickens for meat or for more than one purpose, the bigger the better, I say. Although they will take longer to reach maturity, the wait is worth it.

Hardy: Let's face it—accidents are just going to happen, especially if you have animals or children. It wouldn't be the first time a dog mows down a couple of chickens as it chases a plane or a toddler grabs a chicken by the tail—life, and death, happens. Large chicken breeds are hardier and can withstand a licking and keep on ticking.

CONS OF LARGE CHICKEN BREEDS

Take longer to reach full size: If you are raising chickens for meat, you may want a fast-growing chicken, such as the Cornish Cross (see page 57), that reaches butcher weight in nine weeks. However, if you want a dual-purpose breed that is huge, one of the large breeds might be a better choice.

Require more living space: Just as large dogs need large dog-houses, large chickens need more living space. When you have a bird with an average weight of 12 to 15 pounds and a height up to 30 inches, perches must be farther apart, nesting boxes should be a little wider, and they'll need plenty of room to move and breathe. Typically, our chickens (average size of five to seven pounds) will fit four to a perch, unless someone is vying for the top of the pecking order. Birds of around 15 pounds tend to fit only two to a perch. Chickens that don't have enough space in the coop or in the run tend to develop health issues and fight more among themselves.

Require more food: More body mass means more feed. For example, an egg-laying chicken with an average weight of 3.5 pounds will eat about 2.5 pounds of food per week. A larger breed weighing 8 pounds will eat 3.5 pounds of food a week, and it goes up from there.

Cost more to raise: As we've seen, larger breeds require more food and more living space. This equates to more money to raise them than smaller chickens. They may require additional investment, too, such as taller fences.

Skip the bubble bath. Chickens bathe often, but not in the tub. They like to dig in the dirt and take dust baths, which removes oil from their feathers. Their favorite place to do this is a nice spot in the sun.

Shorter life span: Some large chicken breeds, such as the Cornish Cross (see page 57), were bred to grow large for meat production. They grow so big that their legs and organs can't handle their growth rate; their legs can break under their weight, and their organs can give out. Other large breeds were designed for massive egg production. Egg production requires a lot from a hen, and her life expectancy isn't as long as that of a standard chicken.

THE ULTIMATE LARGE CHICKEN LIST

My ultimate large chicken list contains some of the largest breeds of chickens there are. Some breeds are even Guinness World Record winners, such as the Brahma, standing at almost 30 inches tall, and the White Sully (see page 92), weighing in at 23 pounds. Although impressive, not all large breeds are as massive as the two I just mentioned. In some cases, I have cross-referenced birds from other ultimate lists, as they serve multiple purposes.

BRAHMA

Brahmas are sweet, huge heritage breed chickens with feathered feet. They were initially bred for meat production, but they are good

HOW BIG DO CHICKENS REALLY GET?

On record, the largest recorded chicken was 23 pounds, 3 ounces. Off record, a friend of mine says they have two chickens that are almost 30 pounds, but I haven't seen the scale. They *look* more like turkeys than chickens. In addition to chicken breeds that weigh a lot, the Indian Giant (see page 88) has been recorded at 41 inches tall! The Dong Tao breeds have legs that can weigh over two pounds, while the Brahma can get as wide as a human. Breeds this big resemble their dinosaur cousins more than the traditional backyard chickens. All are very impressive chicken breeds and make delightful additions to the chicken enthusiast's flock!

mothers and pets, so they make a great dual-purpose breed. They tolerate the cold weather and are relatively hardy but do not like hot weather as much. Because of their feathered feet, regular inspections are needed to ensure that their feet are in good health, especially if you have a lot of rain or mud. According to the Livestock Conservancy, their status is "recovering."

Origin: United States
Purpose: Meat, eggs
Climate: Cold hardy, prefers dry climates
Temperament: Calm, docile
Average weight: 9.5 to 12 pounds
Average height: 30 inches
Harvest age: 8 to 10 weeks
Egg color: Brown
Egg size: Large
Egg production: About 150 per year
Feather color: Light, dark, buff coloring with black tail feathers and neck feathers
Comb type: Pea

DONG TAO

The Dong Tao chicken must be one of the more unusual breeds of chickens on our list. Also called Dragon Chickens, they are a rare Vietnamese breed. Prized for their meat, which was once only served to royalty, a pair of Dong Tao chickens could cost a couple of thousand dollars. They have unforgettable legs that are stout and thick, about the size of your wrist. The bulkiness of their legs makes it hard for them to breed, and eggs must often be raised in an incubator.

Origin: Vietnam
Purpose: Meat, show
Climate: Heat tolerant, sensitive to weather changes
Temperament: Calm
Average weight: 8.3 to 13.5 pounds
Average height: n/a
Harvest age: 8 months
Egg color: Cream

Egg production: 60 to 70 per year
Feather color: Black-breasted red, wheaten
Comb type: Pea

INDIAN GIANT (ÍNDIO GIGANTE)

The Indian Giant is one of the largest breeds in the world. It was developed in Brazil by breeding an oversized fighting cock and other large breeds, such as the Shamo (see page 91) and Malay (see page 89). They are a highly desired breed for their unique physical traits as well as their large muscle mass and hardiness. Indian Giants are a beautiful breed that commands attention wherever it's present. Any chicken breeder would be fortunate to have this breed in their flock.

Origin: Brazil
Purpose: Meat, show
Climate: Heat tolerant, tropical
Temperament: Docile
Average weight: 10 to 13.2 pounds
Average height: 41 inches
Harvest age: 18 weeks
Egg color: Tan
Egg production: About 160 per year
Feather color: Wide variety
Comb type: Pea

JERSEY GIANT

This breed also made the ultimate meat list (see page 54), since their large size provides lots of meat if you're willing to wait the eight to nine months for them to reach maturity (not uncommon in large breeds). In the late 1800s, brothers Thomas and John Black developed the Jersey Giant with the specific intention of creating a premium table bird that could replace the turkey. Suddenly, their size makes sense! They were admitted to the APA in 1922. According to the Livestock Conservancy, their status is "watch."

Origin: United States
Purpose: Eggs, meat, broody
Climate: Cold hardy

Temperament: Friendly, docile
Average weight: 12 to 16 pounds
Average height: 22 to 26 inches
Harvest age: 8 to 9 months
Egg color: Brown
Egg size: Medium
Egg production: 160 to 200 per year
Feather color: Black
Comb type: Single

LINCOLNSHIRE BUFF

The Lincolnshire Buff originated in Lincolnshire, England, in the mid-1800s. It is a rare breed that was recreated and standardized in the 1980s. Originally, these chickens were bred to be fast-growing, high-quality table birds that were also hardy. They look very similar to Buff Orpingtons (see page 45), which ended up being more popular than the Lincolnshire but have different characteristics. For example, the Lincolnshire Buff has five toes (instead of four), feathered legs, and a buff-colored beak.

Origin: England
Purpose: Eggs, meat, pet
Climate: Tolerates all climates
Temperament: Friendly
Average weight: 8 to 11 pounds
Average height: 12 to 15 inches
Harvest age: 22 weeks
Egg color: Tinted brown
Egg size: Medium to large
Egg production: 120 to 130 per year
Feather color: Buff
Comb type: Single

MALAY

The Malay is one of the tallest breeds of chickens, thanks to its long legs, long neck, and upright stance. It is a game breed and an ancient landrace breed. Malays weren't introduced to the United States until 1846, but they were the first gigantic Asiatic breed to make its presence known in the Western world. They have several idiosyncratic traits. For example, the rooster's crow sounds a bit like a roar, and some say their facial features give them a severe look. According to the Livestock Conservancy, their status is "critical."

Origin: Southeast Asia
Purpose: Meat
Climate: Heat tolerant, tropical
Temperament: Aggressive
Average weight: 7 to 9 pounds
Average height: Up to 36 inches
Harvest age: 14 to 16 weeks
Egg color: Tinted brown
Egg production: About 120 a year
Feather color: Black-breasted red
Comb type: Cushion

MALINE

The Maline is a breed that was developed in the early 1800s in Belgium. Malines are sought after for their high-quality meat and are coveted table birds. They don't like flying and are content being fenced in, making them great for homesteads. Malines are great foragers and will hunt for food from dusk until dawn. The Malines are an endangered breed and adding them to your flock would help preserve them for future generations.

Origin: Belgium
Purpose: Eggs, meat, pet
Climate: Cold hardy, heat tolerant
Temperament: Calm, docile
Average weight: 10 to 12 pounds
Average height: 12 to 16 inches
Harvest age: 10 to 16 weeks
Egg color: Tan
Egg size: Large
Egg production: 140 to 160 per year
Feather color: Black and white herringbone
Comb type: Single

SAIPAN JUNGLE FOWL

Saipan Jungle Fowl is from the island of Saipan in the South Pacific. It's a very slow grower, taking two years or more to reach its full weight, but it's also known as a long-lived breed. The roosters can reach an impressive three feet tall! Raised for cockfighting, the Saipan Jungle Fowl is a rare domestic breed that does well in areas where predators can be an issue. They thrive in tropical climates and don't do well in cold weather. They require a specialized diet of high animal proteins and low amounts of grains and fats, since their forage consists of coastal protein.

Origin: Saipan
Purpose: Broody, meat
Climate: Cold intolerant, heat and humidity tolerant
Temperament: Calm, tame, and assertive
Average weight: 9 to 13 pounds
Average height: 4 to 36 inches
Harvest age: 22 to 26 weeks
Egg color: Cream
Egg production: 40 to 90 per year
Feather color: Black-breasted red with some white and wheaten
Comb type: Pea

SHAMO

Shamo is a heritage breed originally developed in the early 1600s in Thailand and Japan for naked-heel (no spurs) boxing. These chickens were bred for their endurance and strength. Reaching a height of almost 30 inches, the Shamo stands nearly completely erect. It is a great forager but does not do well in confinement. Its meat is said to have a gamy taste and is not preferred by most. The hens tend to go broody and make excellent mothers. According to the Livestock Conservancy, their status is "watch."

Origin: Thailand
Purpose: Broody, game, ornamental
Climate: Heat tolerant
Temperament: Calm and territorial
Average weight: 7.5 to 12.5 pounds

Average height: 30 inches
Egg color: Light brown
Egg production: About 90 per year
Feather color: Black, black-breasted red, dark red
Comb type: Pea

WHITE SULLY

No large chicken breed list would be complete without mentioning the White Sully, also known as the "super bird." The White Sully was developed by Grant Sullens of California by crossbreeding and re-crossbreeding Rhode Island Reds (see page 19), Plymouth Rocks (see page 18), and Austra Whites (see page 44). He developed the White Sully to withstand the cold climate and provide meat and eggs. Grant claimed that his White Sullies were superior to any other fowl in both hardiness and production. They grew fast, and the hens laid all year. The White Sully is the largest breed of chicken on record.

Origin: United States
Purpose: Eggs, meat
Climate: Tolerates most climates
Temperament: Aggressive
Average weight: 23 pounds
Average height: 20 inches
Harvest age: 16 to 24 weeks
Egg color: White
Egg size: Large
Egg production: 300 per year
Feather color: White and various
Comb type: Single

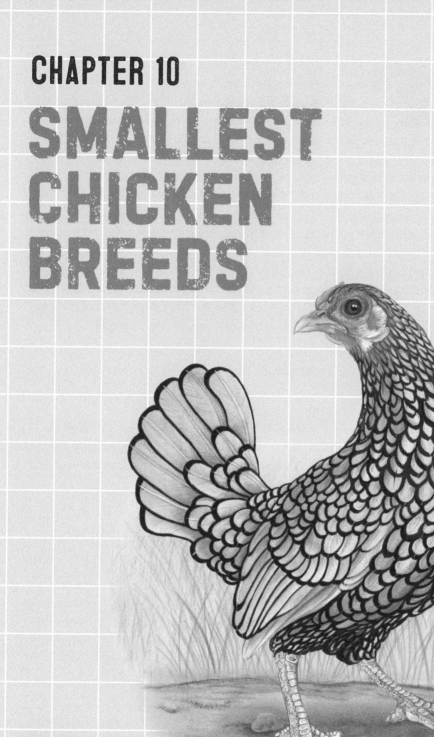

CHAPTER 10
SMALLEST CHICKEN BREEDS

SEBRIGHT;
PAGE 100

For every large breed of chicken that you love, chances are that there is an equally amazing but more adorable smaller breed of the same kind. Small breeds of domestic fowl are called bantams. In many cases, chicken farmers selectively bred standard versions into miniature versions, so several standard breeds have bantam counterparts that are identical in appearance except for their size. However, there are some breeds, called true bantams, that have never had a standard-size counterpart. The Nankin (see page 82) is an example.

Most bantam chicken breeds are under two pounds and stand between nine and 12 inches. Although tiny in stature, they are often great egg-layers, mothers, and show birds, making them sought after by other breeders and a potentially profitable investment. This chapter reviews the pros and cons of keeping small breeds and provides a list of my top small-breed choices for backyard flocks.

PROS AND CONS OF SMALL CHICKENS

You should always go into the decision of adding a breed to your flock with eyes wide open. For that reason, let's take a closer look at the pros and the cons of adding small chickens to your homestead.

PROS OF SMALL CHICKEN BREEDS

Less space: Much like how bigger breeds require more space, smaller breeds require less space. Smaller space requirements mean you can have more chickens, and that's always a good thing!

Cost less to feed: In addition to saving on coop space, small breeds eat less. Whereas a large or standard chicken breed might cost an average of $30 per year per chicken in nonorganic feed, a bantam might cost closer to $10 per year per chicken.

Sell for more money: Who doesn't love a beautiful chicken in a tiny little package? Small chicken breeds are desired by breeders and chicken enthusiasts all over the world. The small chicken business can become quite lucrative. A breeding pair can go for double or triple what their standard-size counterparts go for.

Easier to handle: Little chickens are easier to hold and handle than bigger birds, making their care easier as well.

Less damage to landscape: Chickens can destroy your gardens and flower beds. Trust me. Mine have even gotten good at jumping the fencing I've installed around my gardens. They scratch and peck, love produce, and eat bugs. That's what they do. Smaller birds mean less damage, and that's certainly a benefit.

CONS OF SMALL CHICKEN BREEDS

Don't like confinement: One would think you can raise small birds in small cages or runs; however, bantam breeds don't care for confinement. They are skittish and like to be high up. They enjoy open spaces.

Flight risk: As I previously mentioned, chickens can fly (also see sidebar on page 96). In fact, bantam breeds often fly quite well. However, you can train them to understand that their coop is home or trim their wings to reduce the flight risk.

Hard to acquire: This is a pro and a con. It's a con because it may take a little time to find the bantam you want to purchase. However, it's a pro because once you have a breeding pair you can make money from selling their offspring.

Broody: Another pro and con. If you want to raise baby chicks, you need chickens that go broody to hatch your eggs (unless you have an incubator). However, if you don't want to raise baby chickens or you don't have fertilized eggs, then a chicken that wants to sit on eggs all day for days on end can become a pain to deal with.

Easy prey: Let's face it—chickens are pretty much at the bottom of the food chain. Everything likes to eat them, including us! Unfortunately, smaller birds are easier for predators to pick off from above, easier to pull through a fence—they're just easier to grab, all around. Good fencing, security, and a livestock guardian will help with this.

Smaller eggs and less production: Smaller chickens mean smaller eggs. Very few, if any at all, can go head-to-head with standard-size egg-laying breeds. If you want chickens just for the eggs, small breeds may not be for you. However, if you don't consume that many eggs, then the smaller breeds could be a perfect fit.

THE ULTIMATE SMALL CHICKEN LIST

Small breeds can be a lovely addition to a homestead flock. I've compiled this list of the smallest of the small. They are adorable, tiny, and beautiful in plumage—perfect for showing or selling or as pets. A couple appear on other lists, as they are great for more than one thing.

APPENZELLER SPITZHAUBEN

Switzerland's national bird, the Appenzeller was bred for steep, mountainous terrain. These chickens are great fliers and foragers. If the land provides, they will forage for all their dietary needs. They like to roost in trees. Appenzellers have a crested top hat and beautiful white and black feathers. They are a heritage breed that is recognized in Europe, but they are not yet recognized by the APA.

Origin: Switzerland
Purpose: Eggs, show
Climate: Cold hardy
Temperament: Active, flighty

CAN SMALL CHICKENS FLY?

All chickens can fly, although some are better than others. Chickens need a proper wing-to-weight ratio in order to fly. Chickens require one inch of wing mass per .06 ounces of body weight to fly. While most of the larger chicken breeds don't meet these criteria, some of the smaller breeds do. In fact, some of the smaller breeds can fly quite well. You can clip their wings (trim their flight feathers) to contain them in a fenced-in yard to prevent flying.

Average weight: 3.5 to 4.5 pounds
Egg color: White
Egg size: Medium
Egg production: About 156 per year
Feather color: Silver spangled
Comb type: V-shape

BOOTED BANTAM (SABELPOOT)

Booted Bantams, or Sabelpoot in Dutch, are foragers and do little damage to landscapes. They have stunning plumage with wings that point down and feathered feet. They tend to go broody and are respectable egg-layers for a small breed. Popular in Europe, the Booted Bantam was recognized by the American Poultry Association in 1879.

Origin: Netherlands
Purpose: Show, pet
Climate: Moderate, no extremes
Temperament: Friendly, docile
Average weight: Less than 2 pounds (22 to 26 ounces)
Egg color: White tinted
Egg production: About 160 per year
Feather color: Barred, black, blue, buff, cuckoo, Columbian, gray, golden neck, mille fleur, mottled, partridge, lavender, lemon, blue, white
Comb type: Single

D'ANVERS

D'Anvers, also called a Belgian Bantam, is one of the oldest true bantam breeds. The earliest record of the breed dates from 1858. They tolerate all climates and make great mothers. Belgian Bantams are one of the only bantam breeds that are not at serious risk of becoming endangered. The hens love to go broody and are extremely friendly, which makes them perfect pets, especially for those with children. However, the roosters can be aggressive.

Origin: Belgium
Purpose: Show, broody, pet
Climate: Tolerates all climates

Temperament: Friendly, aggressive
Average weight: Less than 2 pounds (22 to 26 ounces)
Egg color: Cream
Egg production: About 150 per year
Feather color: Buff, black-breasted red, quail, blue quail, blue, Columbian, buff Columbian, black, self-blue, mottled, cuckoo, mille fleur, white
Comb type: Rose

DUTCH BANTAM

Dutch Bantams are a true bantam, meaning they do not have a standard-size counterpart. The Dutch Bantams were standardized in the Netherlands in 1906 but are said to have originated in the Riau Islands Province of Indonesia in the 1600s. They are one of the smallest of the true bantams. While their tiny stature doesn't make them a great breed for cold climates, they do make great mothers.

Origin: Netherlands
Purpose: Pet, show, broody
Climate: Cold hardy, heat tolerant
Temperament: Flighty, friendly
Average weight: Less than 2 pounds (15 to 19 ounces)
Egg color: Light brown
Egg production: About 160 per year
Feather color: Partridge, golden duckwing, silver duckwing, blue duckwing, cuckoo, blue golden, self-blue, others
Comb type: Single

MALAYSIAN SERAMA BANTAM

Meet one of the tiniest breeds of chickens in the world. Although they are said to have originated in Malaysia in the 1600s, they didn't become popular in the United States until the year 2000. You haven't met adorable until you've come face-to-face with one of these one-pound chickens! While they do require some extra care because they are so small, I'd say it's worth it.

Origin: Malaysia
Purpose: Pet, show
Climate: Cold hardy and heat tolerant (nothing below 40 degrees)

Temperament: Friendly
Average weight: Less than 1 pound (6 to 12 ounces)
Egg color: White to deep brown
Egg production: About 120 per year
Feather color: Varied
Comb type: Single

PHOENIX BANTAM

The Phoenix is known for its long tail feathers (that can get as long as 20 feet!) and beautiful saddle feathers. They are a majestic-looking bird. Phoenix Bantams are ornamental birds and not specifically bred for meat or egg production. Because of their special feathers, the breed requires special care. Although this breed has long been bred in Japan, it is still relatively rare in the United States, though it is recognized by the APA.

Origin: Germany, standardized in Japan
Purpose: Eggs, broody, pet, show
Climate: Cold hardy, heat tolerant
Temperament: Active
Average weight: Less than two pounds (28 to 30 ounces)
Egg color: Cream tinted
Egg production: 60 to 120 per year
Feather color: Gold, silver, black, golden duckwing, silver duckwing
Comb type: Single

ROSE COMB BANTAMS

The Rose Comb Bantam is another true bantam with no standard size counterpart. The most popular color has black feathers with a rose comb and white rounded earlobes. These chickens tolerate confinement but love to spread their wings and fly. They aren't recommended for first-time chicken owners but are better suited to the more experienced breeder.

Origin: Great Britain
Purpose: Show, pet
Climate: Cold hardy (with special care to their combs), heat tolerant
Temperament: Friendly

Average weight: Less than 2 pounds (20 to 22 ounces)
Egg color: Cream or tinted
Egg production: About 50 per year
Feather color: Black, blue, white
Comb type: Rose

SEBRIGHT

Sebright first appeared in England in the early 1800s and was developed by John Sebright. It's one of the oldest recorded British bantam breeds. Sebrights are a heritage breed and were recognized by the APA in 1874. They are truly ornamental birds, with the males and the females having almost the exact same feathering, which is highly unusual. They can be difficult to raise due to their limited laying capacity and a lack of broodiness in the hens. According to the Livestock Conservancy, their status is "threatened."

Origin: England
Purpose: Show, pet
Climate: Tolerates all climates
Temperament: Friendly, active
Average weight: Less than 2 pounds (20 to 22 ounces)
Egg color: White
Egg production: About 52 per year
Feather color: Gold silver
Comb type: Rose

SILKIE BANTAM

The Silkie Bantam, which also made the beginner's list (see page 31), is one of the friendliest chicken breeds you will ever own. Their feathers are silken and fluffy. They have five toes, instead of the common four, and feathered feet. Silkie Bantams have a feather crest on their head and grow down on their face. They look like a tiny fluffy cotton ball that lays eggs.

Origin: China
Purpose: Eggs, show, pet
Climate: Cold hardy, heat tolerant
Temperament: Calm, friendly

Average weight: 1.5 to 3 pounds
Egg color: Cream, tinted
Egg size: Small
Egg production: About 100 per year
Feather color: Black, blue, buff, gray, partridge, white
Comb type: Walnut

SULTAN BANTAM

Sultan Bantams enjoy confinement and aren't good foragers. They are very domesticated and like to be pampered. The bantam version of the Sultan breed was developed in the United States in 1960 and is recognized by the American Poultry Association. These chickens have feathered feet and crested heads with fluffy feathers.

Origin: United States
Purpose: Show, pet, broody
Climate: Cold hardy, heat tolerant, intolerant to wet weather
Temperament: Friendly, docile, calm
Average weight: Less than two pounds (20 to 22 ounces)
Egg color: White
Egg production: About 50 per year
Feather color: Black, blue, white
Comb type: V-shape

Chickens make different sounds. Chickens talk all the time and can make up to 30 different sounds—from a purr like a cat to sounds like dinosaurs—which they use to communicate with the other members of the flock.

CHAPTER 11

BEST CHICKENS FOR PETS

SAPPHIRE GEM;
PAGE 109

hen people think of adding chickens to their homestead, they generally want to raise them for eggs or meat. Sometimes, they consider adding chickens to help monetize their homestead or even get into showing chickens. But others decide to raise chickens simply as pets.

Chickens are very social and intelligent, and they generally love to interact with humans. If you're the one who feeds them, they will look to you as their leader. It's no wonder many people raise them as pets. If you're looking for a pet chicken, contact a local farmer and inquire about adopting some hens that are past their prime in egg production. As you've learned, chickens lay eggs at full production for only two to three years; however, many breeds have an average life span of 10 years. Sometimes, people who raise chickens only for egg production look for new homes for their aging hens that still have many years of companionship left in them.

This chapter focuses on breeds that tend to have great personalities and make great pets. We'll explore the basics of raising well-behaved chickens, and then I'll share my list of the top breeds that make great pets on your homestead.

HOW TO RAISE A GOOD PET

In all the years I've been raising chickens, I've found no matter the breed, it was best to raise chickens from baby chicks. They see me as their caregiver and the one who feeds them. Once they know that I am the one who feeds them, they follow me around the yard like I'm the pied piper. As they age, chickens will establish their own pecking order. Although you lack feathers, you are also included in that pecking order. Your chickens will either respect your position or see you as a threat and want to challenge you.

Training chickens with rewards for good behavior is always helpful. For example, I always train my chickens where home (aka their chicken coop) is by keeping them locked in their coop with food and water for two weeks. Then when they have free range of the property, I get some mealworms, place them in a can, and shake it when I want them to go in their coop.

Eventually, they learn to associate the sound of the mealworms can with getting a treat, so they come find me. Now they will follow me and that can of worms anywhere I want them to go. Even if I don't have the can, they come a-running when they see me. To them, I am their worm queen. Chickens have a great memory; they can recognize faces and sounds. I've never met a chicken that doesn't like and respond well to worm treats.

In addition to giving them treats for good behavior, you need to correct bad behavior. Whenever a chicken shows signs of aggression, the best cure is to kill them with kindness—and dominance. Let's say your chicken tries to attack you from behind or come at you. You need to carry that chicken around and hold it close in your arms for at least a good five minutes. Parade it around in front of all its peers to let the chicken, and its peers, know that *you* are the king of the pecking order.

Despite your best efforts, if you have a chicken or a rooster that just continues to display bad behavior or aggression, it's time to move on. Get some water boiling and make chicken soup for the winter months. I never recommend trying to rehome an aggressive rooster—you don't want to dump your problems on someone else. There are too many nice chickens out there to keep one that doesn't fit well on the homestead.

THE ULTIMATE PET CHICKEN LIST

In many species, there are breeds that tend to be nicer than others. Some breeds are skittish and jumpy, while others are laid back and playful. Chicken breeds are much the same way. There are always individuals that buck the tendencies of their breed, and there are days when even the most submissive animal is feeling off. Even though the breeds I list here tend to have docile personalities, they are still animals and unpredictable. Never leave a child alone with an animal, and never let your guard down.

Another thing to keep in mind is that males and females often display different behavior. With some breeds, like bantams, the females tend to be quite friendly, while the roosters are aggressive. I always say life is too short for cheap wine and mean chickens.

BARRED PLYMOUTH ROCK BANTAM

This breed's full-sized version, the Plymouth Rock (see page 18), made a previous ultimate list, and they tend to have similar personalities. The bantam is a sweet, docile, and friendly chicken—full of personality in a tiny package. They are great layers of mini eggs and make good mothers. Their colors—the barred black and white—are iconic. This breed is a staple of chicken owners across the nation and a true American heritage breed.

Origin: United States
Purpose: Eggs, show, pet
Climate: Cold hardy, heat tolerant
Temperament: Docile, friendly
Average weight: Less than 2 pounds (28 to 32 ounces)
Egg color: Brown
Egg size: Small
Egg production: About 156 per year
Feather color: Barred
Comb type: Single

BOVAN NERA

The Bovan Nera does well in both coops and free range. These chickens are an outstanding egg-laying and table breed from Holland. Docile and friendly, they are hardy in all climates and disease resistant. They are well known for their shell quality and foraging. They are a very adaptable and easy-to-manage breed, making them great additions to backyard flocks.

Origin: Scotland
Purpose: Eggs, meat, pet
Climate: Cold hardy, heat tolerant
Temperament: Friendly
Average weight: 8.3 to 8.5 pounds
Harvest age: 14 to 16 weeks
Egg color: Brown
Egg size: Large
Egg production: About 330 per year
Feather color: Black with green and a red throat
Comb type: Single

BURMESE

The Burmese is a true bantam, meaning it doesn't have a standard-size counterpart. Weighing in at just about one pound, these feathered friends are like little pocket pets. Very friendly and easy to tame, the Burmese bantams became almost extinct in the early 20th century but have since made a comeback. They have booted legs (feathered) and a feather crest and can be bearded but are not always. They are great mothers and tend to go broody.

Origin: Myanmar (formerly known as Burma)
Purpose: Pet, show, broody
Climate: Cold hardy
Temperament: Friendly, docile
Average weight: 1 to 1.5 pounds
Egg color: Brown
Egg production: 80 to 120 per year
Feather color: White
Comb type: Single

COLUMBIAN BLACKTAIL

The Columbian Blacktail is the perfect breed for the backyard farmer. These chickens are hybrids of Rhode Island Reds (see page 19) and two strains of Light Sussex. Their offspring is sex-linked, which means they can be sexed at birth by color. They are a hardy breed that does well in the winter as well as the summer. Friendly, easy to manage, and prolific layers, these dual-purpose birds will make any owner happy.

Origin: United Kingdom
Purpose: Eggs, meat, pet
Climate: Cold hardy, heat tolerant
Temperament: Friendly, docile
Average weight: 5 to 6 pounds
Harvest age: 14 to 16 weeks
Egg color: Light brown
Egg size: Large
Egg production: 320 to 340 per year
Feather color: Brown with black tail and wing tips
Comb type: Single

CREAM LEGBAR

The Cream Legbar is a fairly new British breed that has been around for less than 100 years. However, it has quickly become one of the world's most popular autosexing breeds, which means you can tell males and females apart at birth by their marks (as opposed to their coloring, as with sex link breeds). Part of their appeal is their lovely blue eggs, but they also tend to be sociable, easy to handle, and good foragers. Although the Poultry Club of Great Britain has recognized the Cream Legbar since 1958, they are not currently recognized by the APA.

Origin: United Kingdom
Purpose: Eggs, meat, pet
Climate: Cold hardy, heat tolerant
Temperament: Friendly, docile
Average weight: 6 to 7.5 pound
Harvest age: 18 weeks
Egg color: Blue
Egg size: Medium
Egg production: About 230 per year
Feather color: Gold, silver, cream
Comb type: Single

LINCOLNSHIRE BUFF

The Lincolnshire Buff also made our ultimate large breed list (see page 86), but its easy-to-raise nature makes the breed a no-brainer for this list as well. These chickens are hardy, have wonderful personalities, and are able to brood their own chicks. As a bonus, they also are great layers and make good table birds as well.

Origin: England
Purpose: Eggs, meat, pet
Climate: Tolerates most climates
Temperament: Docile, friendly
Average weight: 8 to 11 pounds
Harvest age: 22 weeks
Egg color: Tinted brown
Egg size: Medium to large

Egg production: 120 to 130 per year
Feather color: Buff
Comb type: Single

MILLE FLEUR D'UCCLE BANTAM

The Mille Fleur d'Uccle Bantam has booted legs and a beard and is under two pounds. Their name means "a thousand flowers," and they look like a flock of feathers from head to toe. They were added to the American Poultry Standard of Perfection in 1914 and are a wonderful addition to any flock. As with many bantams, they are calm, sweet chickens that make great pets. They are also a great choice for children learning to raise chickens.

Origin: Belgium
Purpose: Eggs, pet, show
Climate: Cold hardy
Temperament: Calm
Average weight: Less than 2 pounds (22 to 26 ounces)
Egg color: White tinted
Egg size: Small
Egg production: About 160 per year
Feather color: Barred, black, blue, buff, Columbian, cuckoo
Comb type: Single

CAN I KEEP JUST ONE CHICKEN AS A PET?

Chickens are social creatures. While they do make good pets, they need to have other chickens around. They thrive on the activity of their flock. They signal to each other about danger, when to roost, and where the best food is and even stimulate each other to lay eggs. It is essential to their well-being to raise more than just one chicken—I strongly suggest raising no fewer than three chickens. That way if something happens to one, you still have two chickens.

PEKIN

Pekin is a true bantam from China from the early nineteenth century. It is a miniature breed with elaborate feathers and a rounded body, making these chickens a great visual addition to the yard and well suited to showing. They are very docile and curious, and they tend to enjoy socializing with humans. They make great pets, especially for families.

Origin: China
Purpose: Eggs, pet, show
Climate: Tolerates all climates
Temperament: Docile
Average weight: 1 to 1.5 pounds
Egg color: White
Egg size: Small
Egg production: 50 to 100 per year
Feather color: Black, blue, buff, cuckoo, barred, Columbian, lavender, partridge, white
Comb type: Single

SAPPHIRE GEM

Not much is known about the origins of this fairly new breed (which is not yet recognized by the APA), but Sapphire Gems are growing in popularity due to their charming personalities and good looks. These birds tend to be extremely calm and manageable and enjoy spending time with their keepers. They are also beautiful, having light and dark gray feathers with a blue tint. The Sapphire Gem is an excellent layer and forager that does well in both hot and cold climates. It is a sex link, which means its gender can be determined at birth based on its color.

Origin: Czech Republic
Purpose: Eggs, meat, pet
Climate: Tolerates all climates
Temperament: Friendly
Average weight: 4 to 5 pounds
Harvest age: 16 to 22 weeks
Egg color: Brown

Egg size: Large
Egg production: About 290 per year
Feather color: Blue, lavender, light gray, dark gray
Comb type: Single

SICILIAN BUTTERCUP

The Sicilian Buttercup, as the name suggests, has a unique buttercup comb that looks like a crown and white earlobes. It is one of the only breeds with green legs. This Mediterranean heritage breed was bred with egg production in mind, but it makes an excellent medium-sized table bird as well. Active foragers, Buttercups are friendly and have been bred in the United States since the early 1800s. According to the Livestock Conservancy, their status is "watch."

Origin: Sicily
Purpose: Eggs, meat, pet
Climate: Heat tolerant
Temperament: Friendly, active
Average weight: 4 to 5.5 pounds
Harvest age: 16 to 20 weeks
Egg color: White
Egg size: Small
Egg production: About 180 per year
Feather color: Red orange, black tail, buff
Comb type: Buttercup

CHAPTER 12
BEST SHOW CHICKENS

SILVER LACED
WYANDOTTE;
PAGE 118

**W**hile egg-layers and meat birds usually top the list in terms of goals for raising chickens, many chicken keepers are also interested in show chickens. There are several different categories of show chickens, such as heritage, largest, smallest, meat, and egg. Shows are often hosted through 4-H events and county fairs—great places for the family to get involved—and other shows are hosted by the American Poultry Association and breed clubs all over the United States.

In some poultry shows, the winning chickens in each category are auctioned off, and the proceeds go to the winners. A friend of mine raises meat chickens for show for her children, and they have won several thousand dollars toward their college fund.

This chapter focuses on show chickens. We'll cover the basics of preparing and presenting show chickens, and then I'll provide my list of the top show chickens to raise on your homestead.

WHAT DOES IT TAKE TO RAISE SHOW CHICKENS?

Not every chicken is suitable for showing. First, unless you are interested in market shows (see page 114), most shows only deal with purebred chickens (see page 113), so your chickens must have documented lineage. They also must conform to the standards of their breed. That means if you have a purebred chicken, but they have a trait that does not conform to standard, they likely won't do well at a show. These are called "nonconforming" chickens.

How do you know what the standards are? A good place to start is by looking at the regulations and standards for the different breeds of chickens with an organization such as the American Poultry Association (APA). The APA regularly updates and publishes the *American Standard of Perfection*, which describes 19 classes of poultry, 11 of which are chickens. Each class contains the several breeds that fall into that class. Its breed standards will help guide you in understanding what officials look for in a breed. In order to win shows, chickens must tick all the boxes as close to perfection as possible.

Show chickens must also be raised differently than your other chickens. For example, you must keep your purebreds separate so you don't end up with hybrid chickens. It's also recommended that you don't let them range or socialize with other birds, as each can lead to accidents and damage that will hurt the bird's chances at the show. You don't want your prize chickens breaking a leg in the yard or losing feathers to the pecking of a more dominant bird.

Raising chickens for show is a great project and hobby for children and adults alike. Back in the day, the owner who had the blue-ribbon chicken was the talk of the town and still is in many smaller communities. Not only does a prize chicken provide income, but it can also help establish you as a reputable breeder.

CHICKEN SHOWS

When showing chickens, you generally have two different types of shows, breed shows and market shows. Also, shows may differ from state to state. Let's take a closer look at what you can expect in general from both.

BREED SHOWS

Mainly only purebred chickens can be shown for breed shows. However, breeds that are not recognized by the APA or ABA can place for best breed (BB) or rare breed (RB) as well as be entered in other contests such as 4-H and local fairs. You can contact your local extension agency to inquire about local shows and their specific criteria. *The American Standard of Perfection* or the American Bantam Association will be your guide to what each breed should look like and what the judges are looking for in a specific breed. Each breed will have its own standard by which it will be judged.

Breeds will be judged on:

Shape: A chicken must be strong, hardy, and physically fit.

Size: The size of a chicken must comply with the breed standards.

Type: Each breed will have its own category, including male and female.

Color: Color must conform to the APA or breed standards, and the feathers must be clean and undamaged.

Combs: Combs should be vibrant in color, clean, and moisturized.

Wattles: Wattles should be vibrant in color, clean, and moisturized.

Feet: Feet should be clean and free from any injuries or parasites.

Eggs: Eggs are judged on shape, weight, shell color, and uniformity.

In general, shows offer separate categories for roosters, hens, pullets, and cockerels.

MARKET SHOWS

Market shows are much different than breeding shows. At market shows, your chickens are judged by meat yield rather than breed standard. In other words, the judges are looking at the bird from a perspective of the quality and size of the meat cuts, not as a representative of a particular breed. If your meat bird does not confirm to the standards of its breed, it doesn't matter.

TIPS TO GETTING YOUR CHICKENS READY FOR THE BIG DAY

When it's showtime, you want to put your best foot forward—or should I say best feather? When you show your chickens, they will be handled by the judges *a lot*. There will be a lot of people, lights, and noise. This can cause tremendous amounts of stress to your birds if they aren't used to it.

You should train your chickens from a young age to be handled by various people. Their feet, beak, and wings will be examined and touched. Scrub their feet and toes, give them baths, and, above all, keep their bedding clean and changed. Clean bedding helps keep chickens clean.

A couple of days before the competition, add some electrolytes to your chicken's water, and then do so again on the show day. Again, competitions can be stressful, and you want to make sure your feathered friend is in tip-top shape.

On show day, you can add a little olive or coconut oil to the chicken's legs, beak, comb, and wattles, massaging it in for a nice, pretty shine.

THE ULTIMATE SHOW CHICKENS LIST

Chickens from all over the world are stunning works of art. Selective breeding for hundreds of years has turned out some of the most amazing and incredible breeds. You will see all the categories in this book covered in shows—egg production, meat production, large, small, heritage, and plumage. While all chickens are quite impressive, some breeds are just showstoppers. This list of the ultimate show chickens will highlight these breeds. Make note that the breeds that I cover here are specific to breed shows, not market shows.

ASEEL (OR ASIL)

The Aseel also made the best broody list (see page 76). As the world's oldest game fowl, these chickens are held in high regard as "pure" or "thoroughbred" (the English translation of their name), even among heritage breeds, and have garnered a great deal of respect. They have an exotic, fierce look and a very muscular, compact frame. Although the breed is known to be quite aggressive toward other chickens, they tend to be much more docile toward their keepers. According to the Livestock Conservancy, their status is "threatened."

Origin: India
Purpose: Meat, broody, show
Climate: Cold hardy, prefers dry environment
Temperament: Aggressive
Average weight: 4 to 5.5 pounds
Harvest age: 6 to 8 months
Egg color: Cream
Egg size: Small
Egg production: About 40 per year
Feather color: Black-breasted red (wheaten), dark, spangled, white; game colors, such as gray, blue-breasted red, and black. Many color variations have a metallic luster or sheen.
Comb type: Pea

Chickens can be therapy animals. Although chickens aren't typically associated with being therapy animals, they can be recognized as one. They are very affectionate and full of personality.

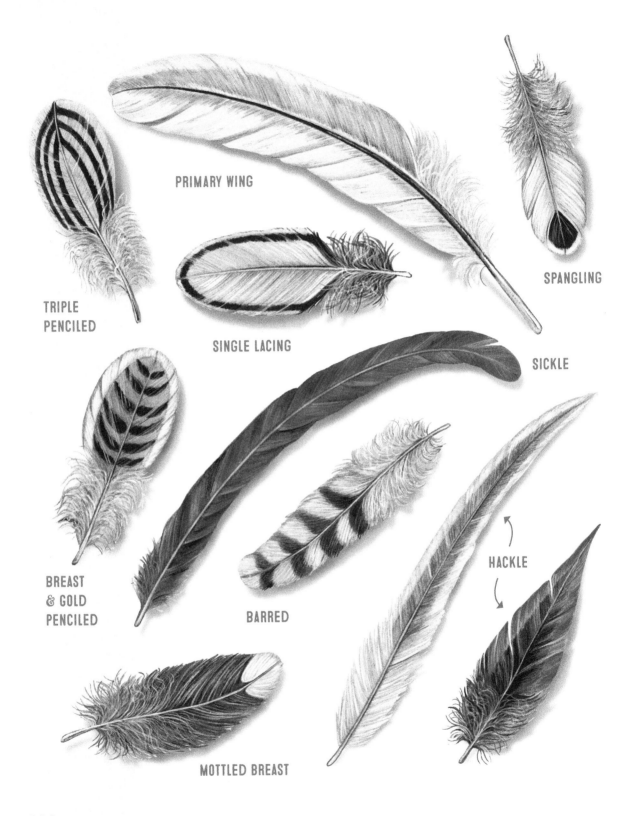

TRIPLE
PENCILED

PRIMARY WING

SPANGLING

SINGLE LACING

SICKLE

BREAST
& GOLD
PENCILED

BARRED

HACKLE

MOTTLED BREAST

AYAM CEMANI

Possibly one of the most sought-after breeds of late, the Ayam Cemani is a truly stunning breed. These chickens are all black: the feathers, beak, wattle, comb, and internal organs! They have a dominant gene that causes hyperpigmentation. Although the Ayam Cemani is not a recognized APA breed, the Ayam Cemani Breeders Association is working hard to develop a standard of perfection. You can still show these birds in best breed (BB) or rare breed (RB) categories as well as in other contests such as 4-H and local fairs. It is a rare and expensive breed that commands attention from everyone in the room. (For a more cold-tolerant version of the Ayam Cemani, check out the Svarthöna, a similar breed.)

Origin: Indonesia
Purpose: Meat, show, pet
Climate: Cold hardy, heat tolerant
Temperament: Docile, friendly
Average weight: 4.4 to 6.6 pounds
Harvest age: 22 to 25 weeks
Egg color: Cream
Egg size: Small
Egg production: About 80 per year
Feather color: Black
Comb type: Single

HOUDAN

The Houdan is a beautiful ancient breed that was first recognized by the APA in 1874. Over the years, Houdans have been respected for their meat production and qualities, but their look is also quite striking. They have stunning black and mottled white plumage, with a beard, crest, and feathered head that demand attention. This unusual appearance makes them stand out in any show. According to the Livestock Conservancy, their status is "threatened."

Origin: France
Purpose: Show, pet
Climate: Cold hardy
Temperament: Friendly, sweet

Average weight: 4.8 to 5.5 pounds
Egg color: White
Egg size: Medium
Egg production: About 150 per year
Feather color: Mottled white on black
Comb type: V-shape

LAKENVELDER

The Lakenvelder breed is a beautiful heritage chicken from Holland that dates back to the early 1700s (although some claim its history dates back much further). This is an attractive show breed with stark contrasting black and white colors (also known as "Shadow on a Sheet"), blue legs, and a flowing tail. These chickens are also great egg-layers, and although they don't produce a lot of meat, it's said to be distinctly tasty. According to the Livestock Conservancy, their status is "threatened."

Origin: Holland
Purpose: Eggs, show
Climate: Tolerates all climates
Temperament: Active, wary
Average weight: 4 to 5 pounds
Harvest age: 16 to 20 weeks
Egg color: White-tinted cream
Egg size: Medium
Egg production: 160 per year
Feather color: Silver, black hackles and black tail feathers with a white middle and a small amount of black-tipped feathers on the wing
Comb type: Single

SILVER LACED WYANDOTTE

The Wyandotte (see page 21) made the best purebred list, and the Silver Laced variety is one of the most beautiful breeds for showing. Silver Laced Wyandottes are classed as an American breed by the APA. They have beautiful plumage that looks like stained glass. They tolerate both heat and cold and lay eggs through the winter. Bred to be all-around birds, they have lived up to their purpose: great egg-layers, good meat quality and size, friendly and docile, and stunning in shows. They were taken off the Livestock Conservancy's endangered list in 2016.

Origin: United States
Purpose: Show, pet
Climate: Cold hardy
Temperament: Docile, friendly
Average weight: 6.5 to 8.5 pounds
Egg color: Brown
Egg production: About 200 per year
Feather color: White feathers with black edging
Comb type: Rose

SILVER LEGHORN

The Leghorn (see page 47) is one of the best-known chicken breeds, but the Silver variety is among the rarest and most prized. Although Silver Leghorns originated in Italy, the color varieties developed in America, Denmark, and Great Britain. This is a very hardy breed in both hot and cold climates. This is a beautiful heritage breed bird that is a prolific layer. According to the Livestock Conservancy, their status is "recovering."

Origin: Tuscany
Purpose: Eggs, show
Climate: Cold hardy, heat tolerant
Temperament: Alert, active
Average weight: 5 to 7 pounds
Egg color: White
Egg size: Medium
Egg production: About 280 per year
Feather color: Silver, white, with greenish black
Comb type: Single and rose

SUMATRA

The Sumatra was originally from the Isles of Sumatra in Indonesia and introduced to the United States in 1847. Sumatras have very distinctive flowing tail feathers that can grow up to four feet in length. They can jump to heights of six feet and are capable of flying. The males are aggressive during breeding season and can have multiple spurs, which are desired for show. The Sumatra was admitted into the *American Standard of Perfection* in the late 1800s and is an excellent breed for show. According to the Livestock Conservancy, their status is "watch."

Origin: Sumatra
Purpose: Show
Climate: Tolerates all climates
Temperament: Flighty, jumpy
Average weight: 4.9 to 5.9 pounds
Egg color: White
Egg production: About 100 per year
Feather color: Blue, black
Comb type: Pea

TURKEN

The Turken also made our best meat breeds list (see page 60), and its large quality and striking appearance are what makes it great for show, too. The APA classifies it under "All Other Breeds." The Turken's neck lacks feathers, giving it the appearance of a turkey, though it has no turkey-related lineage. The lack of feathers is due to a genetic disorder, and the bare skin turns red when exposed to the sun. The Turken is a unique bird and one that captures the attention of onlookers. It is an extremely friendly breed, and Turkens make great mothers, too.

Origin: Romania
Purpose: Eggs, meat, broody
Climate: Cold hardy, heat tolerant
Temperament: Docile, friendly
Average weight: 6 to 9 pounds
Harvest age: 6 months
Egg color: Brown
Egg size: Medium
Egg production: About 100 per year
Feather color: Black, white, buff, red
Comb type: Single

WHITE-FACED BLACK SPANISH

The Spanish (see page 19) made the list of ultimate purebred chickens, and the White-Faced Black variety is among the most striking in the breed. These chickens have beautiful black glossy feathers with a bright red comb and white face. The Spanish is thought to be the oldest breed in the Mediterranean, and it first came to America via Holland in 1825. Due to its origin, it thrives in warm and tropical climates and doesn't do well in cold. It is a decent layer but doesn't go broody often, so eggs should be hatched in an incubator.

Origin: Spain
Purpose: Eggs, show
Climate: Heat tolerant
Temperament: Active
Average weight: 6.5 to 8 pounds
Egg color: White
Egg size: Large
Egg production: About 180 per year
Feather color: Black
Comb type: Single

ARE MY CHICKENS SHOW QUALITY?

If you feel you have a prize chicken, my first suggestion is to reference *The American Standard of Perfection*, otherwise known as the "Chicken Breeders Bible," and confirm that your breed meets all the required standards.

Attend a couple of poultry shows and play spectator. Talk to fellow breeders and, if you're lucky, maybe even a judge. Ask them for advice or the tips of the trade.

Next is to find out show schedules. Many poultry shows are in the summer and fall. If you are choosing to show for market, you'll want to make sure your chickens are at their premium weight by the competition. If you want to enter breed competitions, you'll want to start grooming your chickens in preparation. Fall is also a time when chickens tend to molt (lose their feathers), so having a backup chicken for competition is always a good idea. No need to place all your eggs in one basket, so to speak.

YOKOHAMA

The Yokohama was recognized by the APA in 1981 in two varieties: the White and Red Shouldered. Some say these chickens are like the Sumatra (see page 119). Their look is quite unusual and elegant, featuring beautiful white flowing feathers with long saddle feathers and long tail feathers that cascade to the ground. Red adorns their shoulders and breast, and their tails can grow to be three to four feet long. They are great mothers and love to roam. They do require extra protein in their diet when growing out their tail feathers. According to the Livestock Conservancy, their status is "critical."

Origin: Germany
Purpose: Show
Climate: Heat tolerant
Temperament: Calm
Egg color: Light tinted brown
Egg production: About 50 per year
Feather color: Red saddled (feathers in front of the tail), white
Comb type: Pea or walnut

Raising chickens for show is something the whole family can get in on. Children often begin showing chickens as a part of their 4-H project or county fair. Winners can be awarded college scholarship money and other prizes. As a serious chicken breeder, winning show awards helps establish you as a breeder and places you in higher demand for your chickens. Even if you don't want to show chickens personally, the shows are always fun to attend and observe. Who knows? You may even find a new breed or two you want to add to your flock!

CONCLUSION

Picking the right chicken breeds can be tricky! I get questions all the time from concerned chicken-owners—often about how their hens have stopped laying eggs. In reality, however, the owners are raising a breed that is known for a low egg-production rate, and what they are experiencing is totally normal. When my family lived in a tropical climate, we unknowingly bought a breed that preferred colder temperatures. Now that I have some feather experience behind me, I'm happy to say we currently have seven different breeds that thrive where we live and keep us with a fresh supply of eggs all year long.

I'm glad that I was able to share my wisdom with you here, and I hope you've enjoyed learning about the different chicken breeds' character traits and qualities. Hopefully, after reviewing all of the amazing breeds available, not only will you venture to try raising new breeds, but you will also strive to find ones that will thrive on your homestead. I wish you the best of luck with your flocks!

RESOURCES

American Bantam Association | BantamClub.com

American Poultry Association | Amerpoultryassn.com

Common Sense Home | Commonsensehome.com/homestead-chicken-resources

The Farmer's Lamp | TheFarmersLamp.com/chickens

The Livestock Conservancy | LivestockConservancy.org

My Homestead Life | MyHomesteadLife.com/chickens

Oak Hill Homestead | OakHillHomestead.com

The Rustic Elk | TheRusticElk.com/category/homesteading/raising-livestock

The Self Sufficient HomeAcre | TheSelfSufficientHomeAcre.com

Timber Creek Farm | TimberCreekFarmer.com/category/chickens

REFERENCES

CHAPTER ONE

Jacob, Jacquie. "External Anatomy of Chickens." Small and Backyard Poultry. The Poultry Extension. Accessed October 15, 2020. poultry.extension .org/articles/poultry-anatomy/external -anatomy-of-chickens.

Nutrena. "How Much Does a Chicken Eat?" Accessed October 15, 2020. nutrenaworld.com/blog/how-much -does-a-chicken-eat.

Smith, Kassandra. "Chicken Head Anatomy." *Backyard Chicken Coops*. Last modified July 21, 2020. backyard chickencoops.com.au/blogs/learning -centre/chicken-head-anatomy.

University of Illinois Extension. "Combs." Incubation and Embryology. Accessed October 15, 2020. web.extension .illinois.edu/eggs/res11-combs.html.

US Poultry and Egg Association. "Anatomy and Physiology of Poultry." Accessed October 15, 2020. uspoultry .org/educationprograms/PandEP _Curriculum/Documents/PDFs/ Lesson11/PoultryAnatomyand PhysiologyPres.pdf.

CHAPTER TWO

"11 Reasons You'll Love Chickens." World Animal Protection, October 31, 2020. worldanimalprotection.us/blogs/11 -facts-about-chickens.

Damerow, Gail. "How to Choose: Heritage Breed Chickens." *Hobby Farms*. April 9, 2019. hobbyfarms.com/heritage -breed-chickens-choose.

The Farmer's Lamp. "Saving Heritage Breed Chickens." Accessed October 15, 2020. thefarmerslamp.com/saving -heritage-breed-chickens.

Garman, Janet. "Does It Matter If You Raise Heritage Chicken Breeds or Hybrids?" *Backyard Poultry*. Last updated March 14, 2019. backyard poultry.iamcountryside.com/chickens -101/heritage-chicken-breeds-or -hybrids.

Harrison, John. "Purebred Chickens— What Are Purebred Hens?" *The Poultry Pages*. Accessed October 15, 2020. chickens.allotment-garden.org /keeping-chickens/hybrid-or-pure -breed-chickens/pure-breed-chickens.

Heritage Poultry Conservancy. "Heritage Breeds." *Poultryville*. heritagepoultry .org/poultryville.

Jacob, Jacquie. "Poultry Genetics: An Introduction." Small and Backyard Poultry. The Poultry eXtension. Accessed October 15, 2020. poultry

.extension.org/articles/poultry-anatomy/poultry-genetics-an-introduction.

Kazek, Kelly. "The Battle for the World's Oldest Chicken." April 11, 2018. al.com/living/2018/04/the_battle_for_the_worlds_olde.html.

The Livestock Conservancy. "Conservation Priority List, Chickens." Accessed October 15, 2020. livestockconservancy.org/index.php/heritage/internal/conservation-priority-list#Chickens.

The Livestock Conservancy. "Heritage Chicken." Accessed October 15, 2020. livestockconservancy.org/index.php/heritage/internal/heritage-chicken.

The Livestock Conservancy. "Icelandic Chicken." Accessed October 15, 2020. livestockconservancy.org/index.php/heritage/internal/icelandic.

The Livestock Conservancy. "Plymouth Rock Chicken." Accessed October 15, 2020. livestockconservancy.org/index.php/heritage/internal/plymouthrock.

The Livestock Conservancy. "Quick Reference Guide to Heritage Chickens." Accessed October 15, 2020. livestock

conservancy.org/images/uploads/docs/pickachicken.pdf.

The Livestock Conservancy. "Rhode Island Red—Non Industrial Chicken." Accessed October 15, 2020. livestockconservancy.org/index.php/heritage/internal/rired.

Smith, Kassandra. "Bantams, Bantams, Bantams!" *Backyard Chicken Coops*. Last updated July 17, 2020. backyardchickencoops.com.au/blogs/learning-centre/bantams-bantams-bantams.

Smith, Kassandra. "Hybrid, Heritage, Purebred, or Bantam Chicken Breed?" *Backyard Chicken Coops*. Last updated July 17, 2020. backyardchickencoops.com.au/blogs/thechookcoop/hybrid-heritage-purebred-bantam-chicken-breed.

University of Kentucky College of Agriculture, Food, and Environment. "Small Flocks: Breed Associations and Clubs." Accessed October 15, 2020. afs.ca.uky.edu/poultry/small-flocks-breed-associations-and-clubs#us.

CHAPTER THREE

Chicken Coops Direct. "Choosing the Right Breed of Chicken." Accessed October 16, 2020. chickencoopsdirect.com/breed-guide.pdf.

Clarke, Sue. "A Guide to Pedigree, Purebred, Heritage, and Hybrid Chicken Breeds." *This NZ Life*. Accessed October 16, 2020. thisnzlife.co.nz/guide-pedigree-purebred-heritage-hybrid-chicken-breeds.

Decoriolis, Andrew. "What Is Hybrid Poultry?" *Farm Forward*. Last updated May 15, 2020. farmforward.com/#!/blog?blogid=what-is-hybrid-poultry.

Geggel, Laura. "Forget about the Road. Why Are Chickens So Bad at Flying?" *Live Science*. Last updated December 8, 2016. livescience.com/57139-why-chickens-cannot-fly.html.

The Happy Chicken Coop. "The A-Z of Chicken Breeds and Choosing the Perfect One." Last Modified June 27, 2019. thehappychickencoop.com /chicken-breeds.

The Happy Chicken Coop. "Sussex Chicken: Breed Information, Care Guide, Egg Color and More." Last updated March 21, 2018. thehappy chickencoop.com/sussex-chicken.

The Livestock Conservancy. "Brahma Chicken." Accessed October 16, 2020. livestockconservancy.org/index.php /heritage/internal/brahma.

The Livestock Conservancy. "Cochin Chicken." Accessed October 15, 2020. livestockconservancy.org/index.php /heritage/internal/cochin.

The Livestock Conservancy. "Leghorn— Non Industrial Chicken." Accessed October 15, 2020. livestockconservancy .org/index.php/heritage/internal /leghorn.

The Livestock Conservancy. "Plymouth Rock Chicken." Accessed October 15, 2020. livestockconservancy.org/index .php/heritage/internal/plymouthrock.

The Livestock Conservancy. "Quick Reference Guide to Heritage Chickens." Accessed October 15, 2020. livestock conservancy.org/images/uploads /docs/pickachicken.pdf.

The Livestock Conservancy. "Rhode Island Red—Non Industrial Chicken." Accessed October 15, 2020. live stockconservancy.org/index.php /heritage/internal/rired.

The Livestock Conservancy. "Wyandotte Chicken." Accessed October 15, 2020. livestockconservancy.org/index.php /heritage/internal/wyandotte.

Meyer Hatchery. "Lavender Orpington." Accessed October 16, 2020. meyerhatchery.com/productinfo .a5w?prodID=LAOS.

Oklahoma State University Department of Animal Science. "Poultry Breeds— Cornish Chickens." Accessed October 16, 2020. afs.okstate.edu/breeds /poultry/chickens/cornish/index.html.

Oklahoma State University Department of Animal Science. "Poultry Breeds— Leghorn Chickens." Accessed October 16, 2020. afs.okstate.edu/breeds /poultry/chickens/leghorn/index.html.

Omlet. "Hybrid." Accessed October 16, 2020. omlet.us/breeds/chickens /hybrid.

Perdeaux, Anne. "Hybrid Chickens: The Best Laying Hens?" *Poultry Keeper*. Last updated September 9, 2018. poultrykeeper.com/general-chickens /the-best-laying-hens.

Roberts, Wayne. "The Ultimate Guide to Lavender Orpington Chicken Breed. *Delaney Chicken*. Last updated April 12, 2020. delaneychicken.com/lavender -orpington.

CHAPTER FOUR

"10 Interesting Facts about Chicken Vision- VAL-CO." VAL, December 22, 2017. val-co.com/10-interesting -facts-chicken-vision.

Anger, Rachel Hurd. "6 Gentle Chicken Breeds for Families." *Hobby Farms*. Last updated March 16, 2016. hobbyfarms.com/6-gentle-chicken -breeds-for-families.

Michigan State University. "Chicken Breed Chart to Help Choose Your Chicken." Accessed October 16, 2020. canr.msu.edu/uploads/234/69325 /Chicken_Breed_Chart_to_Help _Choose_Your_Chicken.pdf.

Roper, Kelly. "Pet Chicken Breeds Known for Being Friendly and Docile." *Love to Know*. small-pets.lovetoknow.com/pet -birds/pet-chicken-breeds.

CHAPTER FIVE

4-H Learning Network. "How Many Eggs Can a Chicken Lay in One Day?" Last updated September 4, 2019. 4hlnet .extension.org/how-many-eggs-can -a-chicken-lay-in-one-day.

Brimwood Farm. "Dual Purpose Poultry, Ixworth Chickens." Last updated July 2018. brimwoodfarm.com/articles/2018 /7/8/dual-purpose-poultry-ixworth -chickens.

Damerow, Gail. "How Does an Egg Develop Inside a Chicken?" *Cackle Hatchery*. Last updated January 26, 2017. blog.cacklehatchery.com/how -does-an-egg-develop-inside-a -chicken.

Food and Nutrition. "How Are Eggs Graded by the USDA?" Last updated April 29, 2013. foodandnutrition.org /may-2013/eggs-graded-usda.

Gibbons, Whit. "ECOVIEWS: What Percentage of Animals Lay Eggs?" *Tuscaloosa News*. Last updated January 5, 2020. tuscaloosanews .com/opinion/20200105/ecoviews -what-percentage-of-animals-lay -eggs.

Kiprop, Victor. "Animals that Lay Eggs— Oviparous Animals." *World Atlas*. Last updated October 10, 2018. worldatlas .com/articles/animals-that-lay-eggs -oviparous-animals.html.

Lay Some Eggs. "14 Best Egg Laying Chickens (Chart)." Last updated January 16, 2020. laysomeeggs.com /best-egg-laying-chickens.

Livestock of the World. "About Braekel (Brakel) Chickens." Accessed October 16, 2020. livestockoftheworld.com /chickens/Breeds.asp?BreedLookup ID=2286&SpeciesID=13.

Marengo, Katherine, and James McIntosh. "Everything You Need to Know about Eggs." *Medical News Today*. Last updated October 9, 2019. medicalnewstoday.com/articles /283659#nutrition.

Munn, Dorothy. "Why Are Chicken Eggs Different Colors?" Michigan State University Extension. Last updated December 29, 2020. canr.msu.edu /news/why_are_chicken_eggs _different_colors.

Rääbus, Carol. "Why Some Chickens Lay Brown Eggs and Some Lay Blue, the Chemistry of Eggshell Colour Explained." ABC Radio Hobart. Last updated February 18, 2018. abc.net.au /news/2018-02-19/chemistry-of -eggshell-colour/9455660.

Schaareman, Jan. "Brakel and Brakel Bantams." Aviculture-Europe. Accessed October 16, 2020. aviculture-europe.nl /nummers/11E04A05.pdf.

Science of Cooking. "Anatomy of a Chicken Egg." Accessed October 16, 2020. scienceofcooking.com/eggs /anatomy-of-a-chicken-egg.html.

Shahbandeh, M. "Per Capita Consumption of Eggs in US 2000–2020." *Statista*. Accessed October 16, 2020. statista .com/statistics/183678/per-capita -consumption-of-eggs-in-the-us -since-2000.

US Department of Agriculture. "Shell Egg Grades." Accessed October 16, 2020. ams.usda.gov/grades-standards/egg /grade-shields.

"You Can Determine the Colour of an Egg a Chicken Lays by Looking at It's Earlobe." Office for Science and Society, April 18, 2019. mcgill.ca/oss/article /did-you-know-nutrition/you-can -determine-colour-egg-looking -chickens-earlobe.

CHAPTER SIX

Best Food Facts. "What's the Difference between White and Dark Chicken?" Last updated February 7, 2017. best-foodfacts.org/difference-between -white-dark-chicken.

Liu, Hong-Xiang, Prasangi Rajapaksha, Zhonghou Wang, Naomi E Kramer, and Brett J Marshall. "An Update on the Sense of Taste in Chickens: A Better Developed System than Previously Appreciated." *Journal of Nutrition & Food Sciences* 08, no. 02 (2018).doi .org/10.4172/2155-9600.1000686.

Murdoch's. "Chicken Breed Recom-mender." Accessed October 16, 2020. murdochs.com/learning-center /chickens/chicken-breeds.

National Chicken Council. "Survey Shows US Chicken Consumption Remains Strong." Last updated July 24, 2018. nationalchickencouncil.org/survey -shows-us-chicken-consumption -remains-strong.

US Department of Agriculture Economic Research Service. "Food Availability and Consumption." Accessed October 16, 2020. ers.usda.gov/data-products /ag-and-food-statistics-charting-the -essentials/food-availability-and -consumption.

CHAPTER SEVEN

Armitage, N. "Cinnamon Queen Chickens." Cluckin. July 11, 2020. cluckin.net/cinnamon-queen -chickens.html.

Cackle Hatchery. "Bielefelder Chicken." Accessed November 7, 2020. cackle hatchery.com/product/bielefelder -chicken.

Farmer. "Breeds of Chickens: Master Grays." Accessed November 7, 2020. burea-uinsurance.com/en/breed-of -chickens-master-gray.

Hoover's Hatchery. "Blue Andalusian." Accessed November 7, 2020. hoover shatchery.com/blueandalusian.html.

Livestock of the World. "About Braekel (Brakel) Chickens." Accessed November 7, 2020. livestockoftheworld .com/Chickens/Breeds.asp?Breed LookupID=2286&SpeciesID=13.

Meyer Hatchery. "Columbian Wyandotte." Accessed November 7, 2020. meyer hatchery.com/productinfo.a5w? prodID=CLWS#:~:text=Columbian% 20Wyandotte%20Chickens%20are%20 a,great%20choice%20for%20your%20 homestead.

Peck, Charlie. "The Marsh Daisy—An Overview of the Breed." March Daisy Chickens. Accessed November 7, 2020. marshdaisy.org.uk/home/marsh- daisy-history.

Tractor Supply Co. "Amberlinks." Accessed November 7, 2020. tractor supply.com/out-here_articles _chickens_amberlinks.

CHAPTER EIGHT

Belgian d'Uccle & Booted Bantam Club. "About Our Club." Accessed November 7, 2020. belgianduccle.org.

The Chick Hatchery. "Buff Cochin Bantams." Accessed November 7, 2020. thechickhatchery.com/home/buff -cochin-bantams.

Iowa Agriculture Literacy Foundation. "Life Cycle of a Chicken." Accessed November 7, 2020. iowaagliteracy.org /Article/Life-Cycle-of-a-Chicken.

The Livestock Conservancy. "Aseel Chicken." Accessed November 7, 2020. livestockconservancy.org/index.php /heritage/internal/aseel.

Murray McMurray Hatchery. "Cuckoo Marans." Accessed November 7, 2020. mcmurrayhatchery.com/cuckoo _maran.html.

Murray McMurray Hatchery. "Egyptian Fayoumis." Accessed November 7, 2020. mcmurrayhatchery.com /egyptian_fayoumis.html.

Oklahoma State University Department of Animal Science. "Poultry Breeds— Modern Game Chicken." Accessed November 7, 2020. afs.okstate.edu

/breeds/poultry/chickens/modern
game/index.html.

Red Feather Farm. "Icelandic Chickens
at Red Feather Farm." Accessed

November 7, 2020. redfeatherfarm.net
/heritage-breeds/icelandic-chickens.

CHAPTER NINE

Raising Chickens. "The Saipan Jungle
Fowl." Accessed October 16, 2020.
raising-chickens.org/Saipan-Jungle
-Fowl.html.

Sjøgren, Kristian. "Why Do Headless
Chickens Run?" ScienceNordic,
February 13, 2014. sciencenordic
.com/animals-biology-denmark

/why-do-headless-chickens-run
/1396886.

Weird Universe. "Weirdo the Cat-Killing
Superchicken." Accessed October 16,
2020. weirduniverse.net/blog
/comments/weirdo_the_cat_killing
_superchicken.

CHAPTER TEN

American Bantam Association.
"Recognized Breed and Variety."
Accessed October 16, 2020. bantam
club.com/recognized-breed-and
-variety.

Irvine, Kim. "10 of the Smallest Chicken
Breeds." Domestic Animal Breeds. Last

updated November 16, 2018. domestic
animalbreeds.com/10-of-the-smallest
-chicken-breeds.

Meyer Hatchery. "Silver Spangled
Appenzeller Spitzhauben." Accessed
October 16, 2020. meyerhatchery.com
/productinfo.a5w?prodID=GSPS.

CHAPTER ELEVEN

American Buttercup Club. "About the
Breed." Accessed October 16, 2020.
americanbuttercupclub.org/about
-the-breed.html.

Bovans. "About the Bovans Black."
Accessed October 16, 2020. bovans
.com/en/product/bovans-black.

Cackle Hatchery. "Barred Rock Bantam."
Accessed October 16, 2020. cackle
hatchery.com/barred-rock-bantams
.html.

"Can My Chicken Be an Emotional
Support Animal?" ESA Doctors, July 27,
2020.esadoctors.com/emotional
-support-chicken.

Greenfire Farms. "Cream Legbar."
Accessed October 16, 2020. green
firefarms.com/cream_legbar.html.

Hens, Habibs. "Columbian Blacktails."
Backyard Chickens. Last updated
May 15, 2017. backyardchickens.com
/reviews/columbian-blacktails.11409.

Meyer Hatchery. "Mille Fleur Bearded d'Uccle Bantam." Accessed October 16, 2020. meyerhatchery.com/productinfo.a5w?prodID=MIFBS.

Poultry Keeper. "Lincolnshire Buff Chickens." Accessed October 16, 2020. poultrykeeper.com/chicken-breeds/lincolnshire-buff-chickens.

Rare Breeds Survival Trust. "Burmese." Accessed October 16, 2020. rbst.org.uk/burmese.

Roberts, Jason. "16 Friendliest Chicken Breeds to Keep as Pets." *Know Your Chickens.* Last updated April 25, 2020. knowyourchickens.com/friendliest-chicken-breeds.

Roberts, Wayne. "The Sapphire Gem Chicken: What You Need to Know?" *Delaney Chicken.* Last updated August 10, 2019. delaneychicken.com/sapphire-gem-chicken.

Smith, Kassandra. "5 Reasons to Love Pekin Bantam Chickens." *Backyard Chicken Coops.* Last updated July 17, 2020. backyardchickencoops.com.au/blogs/learning-centre/5-reasons-to-love-pekin-bantam-chickens.

Zielinski, Sarah. "14 Fun Facts About Chickens." Smithsonian.com. Smithsonian Institution, August 31, 2011. smithsonianmag.com/science-nature/14-fun-facts-about-chickens-65848556.

CHAPTER TWELVE

Breed Savers. "Naked Necks—Chickens That Look Like Turkeys." Last updated May 7, 2011. breedsavers.blogspot.com/2011/05/naked-necks-chickens-that-looks-like.html.

Ecopeanut. "Red Star Chickens: Everything You Need to Know." Accessed October 16, 2020. ecopeanut.com/red-star-chickens.

The Happy Chicken Coop. "Ayam Cemani: Breed Information, Care Guide, Egg Color, and More." Last updated March 9, 2018. thehappychickencoop.com/ayam-cemani.

Jacob, Jacquie. "Selecting a Chicken Breed for Small of Backyard Poultry Flocks." The Poultry eXtension. Accessed October 16, 2020. poultry.extension.org/articles/getting-started-with-small-and-backyard-poultry/selecting-birds-to-get-for-a-small-or-backyard-poultry-flock/selecting-a-chicken-breed-for-small-or-backyard-poultry-flocks.

The Livestock Conservancy. "Aseel Chicken." Accessed October 16, 2020. livestockconservancy.org/index.php/heritage/internal/aseel.

The Livestock Conservancy. "Lakenvelder Chicken." Accessed October 16, 2020. livestockconservancy.org/index.php/heritage/internal/lakenvelder.

The Livestock Conservancy. "Sumatra Chicken." Accessed October 16, 2020. livestockconservancy.org/index.php/heritage/internal/sumatra.

The Livestock Conservancy. "Yokohama Chicken." Accessed October 16, 2020. livestockconservancy.org/index.php /heritage/internal/yokohama.

Murray McMurray Hatchery. "Silver Laced Wyandottes." Accessed October 16, 2020. mcmurrayhatchery.com/silver _laced_wyandottes.html.

Murray McMurray Hatchery. "Silver Leghorn." Accessed October 16, 2020. mcmurrayhatchery.com/silver _leghorns.html.

Murray McMurray Hatchery. "White Faced Black Spanish." Accessed October 16, 2020. mcmurrayhatchery.com/white_ faced_black_spanish.html.

Successful Farming. "Top 10 Show Chicken Breeds." Last updated February 12, 2013. agriculture.com /family/living-the-country-life/ top-10-show-chicken-breeds.

University of Florida Institute of Food and Agricultural Sciences. "Selecting Eggs for Show." Accessed October 16, 2020. mysrf.org/pdf/pdf_poultry/p9.pdf.

University of Kentucky College of Agriculture, Food, and Environment. "How Much Will My Chickens Eat?" Accessed October 16, 2020. ca.uky .edu/agcomm/pubs/ASC/ASC191 /ASC191.pdf.

INDEX

ACKNOWLEDGMENTS

A special thanks to the members of my tribe in Old Paths to New Homesteading, especially Robyn Montgomery and Elizabeth Preble for sharing their knowledge.

To my grandparents, for instilling the love of chickens in me. For showing me where food comes from and teaching me how to live a sustainable life, even though it took me a long time to get here.

A special thanks to my daughter Morgan, for always correcting my mistakes and being my biggest cheerleader, and my daughter Linden, who has the patience of a saint.

ABOUT THE AUTHOR

Amber Bradshaw loves raising livestock, growing food in her gardens, and living off-grid in the mountains. She teaches others how to become self-sufficient by making things from scratch that are eco-friendly. When she's not with her animals or in the gardens, you can find her writing.

Bradshaw is the author of *Beekeeping for Beginners* and *The Beginner's Guide to Raising Goats.* She is a former 4-H leader as well as a blogger and public speaker. She and her family filmed the building of their off-grid home for a TV documentary called *Building Off the Grid: Smoky Mountain Homestead.* Bradshaw is happy to share her knowledge with others through public speaking, private instruction, and online at MyHomesteadLife.com.

Chickens are an essential part of her sustainable life on her family's developing farm in the mountains of East Tennessee. Her chickens provide her family with meat and eggs, as well as an income.